Daughter Of The Elm

DAUGHTER OF THE ELM

DAUGHTER OF THE ELM

A Tale of Western Virginia Before the War

BY GRANVILLE DAVISSON HALL

—Seldom a tale
So sad, so tender and so true.
—*Shenstone.*

CHICAGO:
MAYER & MILLER, PRINTERS AND PUBLISHERS
1899

TO

MRS. IRENE A. SAFFORD

MY GRACIOUS FRIEND AND SUMMER NEIGHBOR

WHOSE LITERARY ACUMEN DISCOVERED IN THIS LITTLE WAIF
GRACES INVISIBLE TO LESS FRIENDLY EYES, AND WHOSE
KINDLY FAITH HAS EMBOLDENED ME TO PLACE THE
FOUNDLING ON THE DOORSTEP OF THE
GREAT COMPASSIONATE READING
AMERICAN PUBLIC, THIS
VOLUME IS
GRATEFULLY INSCRIBED

PREFACE.

Thirty-eight years ago, "an old man, broken by the storms" of misfortune and wrong, came to me and with burning eyes and quavering voice begged that I would write down the things he would tell me. He poured out in rude, impassioned speech, much of it with bated breath little above a whisper, a tale of lawlessness that ran through years and culminated in the murder of one of his own blood. The people of whom he spoke and something of the history related by him were already known to me. The notes then taken down from the lips of one who has long since paid the debt of nature were for a long time lost to sight and memory. Lately coming upon them by accident, and reading anew the simple, graphic words, appealing to me thus out of the silence and mists of almost forgotten years, the drama of which the old man's story was a part comes back to me with the vividness of life, and I submit the story of it to that universal tribunal of publicity which can be trusted to award the justice denied elsewhere. There are those yet living who will know how much of this recital is real; and if while rendering justice on the one hand, any intentional injustice should be done on the other, let it be remembered that seldom, even in the republic of letters, are the scales of the blind goddess quite evenly balanced.

As the darkest clouds have a silver lining, so the tragedies of life are nearly always gilded with the diviner drama of Love; and, true to nature, this thread of gold will be found to run through the darker web woven in these pages.

Glencoe, Ill., December 15, 1899.

CHAPTER I.

LOVE'S YOUNG DREAM.

The plighted partner of his future life,
They met, embraced, and sat embowered
In woody chambers of the starry night.
—Pollok.

A cloudless Sabbath in June, when, if ever, come perfect days, had nearly run its appointed course. The sun had dipped behind a great hill in the west, and the lengthening shade had reached across the valley marked by a branch of the upper Monongahela, but still left the woods and fields of the rising landscape on the farther side of the river gilded with the glory of the summer sunset.

Alōng the west bank of the river, half hidden by trees, ran a sandy road that followed the curvings of the stream and the inequalities of the ground; and beside this road a great elm tree, famous far and near for its extraordinary proportions and its magnificent spread of limb and leaf, towered above field and river like some gigantic sentinel left on guard by the departed ages.

An ancient two-storied farmhouse, built of hewed logs, which had seen better days but could never boast of much architectural beauty, stood at the end of a lane a few hundred feet from the river road. Not far away were the farm buildings—stable and barn combined, cribs and pens—all, like the house, originally built of logs, but patched and added to with rough boards; all, like the house again, innocent of paint and gray with time and exposure. Around the house was a lawn of natural beauty, but evidently not an object of much care. Some rose bushes, now in bloom, some unpretending beds of old-fashioned flowers, a few groups of glowing geraniums, indicated the presence of feminine taste and the touch of womanly hands. The fences, garden, and other surroundings had that indescribable aspect of neglect which, while not indicating poverty or attaining to squalor, showed the lack of that sympathetic care and touch that make a home look like the dwelling place of the human domestic virtues. Although the farm to which all these belonged embraced many broad acres of rolling bottom and gently sloping hill, all fertile of soil, it, too, in field and fence, had the same air of neglect and thriftlessness as the buildings and fences about the homestead.

Under the great elm at the foot of the lane, now enclosed by a board fence that helps to make a pig-yard, was then a rough bench made of a large poplar slab, set flat side up, with legs in two-inch auger holes at the corners. This bench — hacked, notched, carved, and scratched with initials—told the story of many an idle hour, of many a perplexed brain that had tried to work out its solutions with the edge of a knife on the helpless slab; of many a rendezvous, perhaps, to concoct villainy; of many a meeting of the gentler sort which had left its memorial in the intertwined initials, like those one so often finds on the smooth bark of the beeches along the river bottoms of this same region. Had this old bench been endowed with a memory and a tongue—or, better still, with the modern witness of a graphophone in concealment—it might have repeated to these later years secrets and legends, dark and otherwise, that would have made material for many a romantic structure.

A few hundred yards up the stream, the river-bed was broken by rugged rocks over which the clear summer flood rippled and murmured as it made its way through the narrow channels to the deeper bed directly opposite the elm, where the smoother waters at that moment reflected the tints of the glowing sky.

Across the river, here three or four hundred feet wide, a small stream came down from the hills to the east and south and turned its little tribute over to this branch of the Monongahela; and on the lower bank of this creek, in sight of the elm, was a ragged cabin with a rude garden about it and a ruder smithy, surrounded by evidences that the tenant divided his time between tinkering and fishing.

On the rough bench under the elm at this hour rests a young girl, slender and graceful of figure, plainly though neatly dressed. The face is brunette, of exquisite loveliness, with dark, lustrous eyes fringed with long, jetty lashes; features regular and delicate; mouth sweet, reserved, and somewhat qualified by a resolute chin. The expression of the face just now is pensive, if not sad, and there is a shade of anxiety and restlessness that finds expression in frequent glances up the river road and across the river. On the other side of the river a path comes down to the brink, where a spreading beech sends its roots to the water's edge and furnishes mooring for a small, flat-bottomed boat chained to a root and equipped with a single paddle.

At times the girl rises and walks along the path under the elm, in her hand a simple straw hat with ribbons to tie under the chin; and she swings the hat by the ribbons as if to find relief from her impatience. Then she seats herself again, and the eyes rove from the river road to the path that ends under the beech on the other side.

Now she catches a glimpse, and now gets a full view, of a youthful, manly figure who walks down past the cottage and smithy and quickens his step as he comes within range of the seat under the elm, crosses the creek on the frail foot bridge, strides over the intervening point, and is quickly under the tree which holds captive the little boat. The girl springs from the seat, runs across the road and down the bank to the edge of the river, and calls his name in a low voice that thrills with the pleasure of seeing him. He replies with a wave of the hand, swiftly unfastens the boat, and, giving it a powerful push, springs into it and seizes the paddle. In two or three minutes the boat grates on the gravel at her feet, and, springing out, he pulls it up on the beach and advances to meet her. At the moment he approaches she looks quickly around, up and down the river and up to the road. Not a creature is in sight, and she turns to him and accepts the kiss which sends the rich color to cheek and brow and lends softness to the dark eyes. They clasp hands and walk thus, hand in hand, up to the seat, where for a few moments they stand conversing in low tones that are not for us to hear. Presently there comes a pause, and they turn and sit down on the bench in a way to suggest that it is an old and dear friend that is deep in their most sacred confidences.

She takes off her hat and holds it on her lap, a little nervous, as if not knowing quite how to begin, while a shade of concern overcasts her face.

"George," she says, at length, "I wanted you to come, and still I hoped you would not."

"Why, Loraine," with a little surprise. "What is it?"

"Because the boys are going out to-night, and they want you to go with them, and I don't want you to go."

"Where are they going, and what is to be done?" he asked.

"I can't find out. None of them will tell me. Lynn has been here since last night, and Lot came down about an hour ago, and when Lynn comes I know there is mischief to be done. They have been in the barn, feeding and rubbing down their horses, cleaning and loading pistols, and making great preparations for something; and they are so excited and mysterious. I overheard Lot say, 'George has got to go; he promised to be here before sundown.' "

"I did half promise," he said, "to go with them to-night, though they did not tell me what they were going after. Lot said he would tell me when I came down. But I can't go; I have nothing to ride. Lize cast a shoe, and father took Bet this morning and went up to Uncle Andy's and will not be home till morning. I would not go anyhow if you did not want me to."

He was not looking at her and did not see the quick flush of pleasure these last words brought into her face.

It was growing dusk. Presently there was a confusion of voices at the house, and a few minutes later the clatter of horses' feet coming down the lane. Four men, one of whom was the girl's brother, rode rapidly down the road. Seeing the figures on the bench, they pulled up abruptly, and, riding close to see who they were, the leader addressed the girl's companion:

"George Holmes, you here! What the —does this mean? Where's your horse?"

The person addressed in this rude fashion rose to his feet, as he replied in a manner slightly apologetic:

"Lize is lame, and the old man rode Bet up to Uncle Andy's. He started this morning before I was up, and mother said he was going to stay all night. I walked down to tell you, and would have been up to the house if I hadn't happened to find Loraine here. You'll have to go without me tonight."

There were black looks on all the faces.

"This is a pretty how-d'ye-do," said the leader. "We will see about this when we come back; there's no time to waste now."

He gave the rein to his horse and dashed up the road, the rest following at a gallop.

There was an interval of silence, each of the pair evidently wrestling with troubled thoughts.

"George," said the girl at last, "where will all this end?"

She shivered a little as she spoke, as if at that instant the shadow of impending calamity passed before her spirit.

"What are we to do? If the boys keep this up, I know it will end in misfortune for all of us."

Tears came into her eyes, and her voice faltered. She looked across the river into the deepening shade of the woods. Her companion did not speak at once.

"God knows," he said, "that I have wished a thousand times that it had never been begun. They all blame me because I don't enter into their plans with as much zeal as they do; and I feel as you do, Loraine, that trouble is on the road and coming our way."

"I have begged Harry," she said, suppressing a sob, "to give up these wild night rides and settle down at home and look after the farm, which needs it; and he seems moved sometimes by what I say; but when Lynn and Lot and the rest get around him and flatter him as their leader, he falls in with anything they propose and is as reckless as the worst of them."

Silence fell with the darkness on the couple sitting in the deep shadow of the great tree. Despite their anxieties, they were too much absorbed in the mutual joy of youthful affection to take much real trouble about anything. One after another the stars came out, and in the dim radiance of the peerless night they remained an hour longer, with only occasional exchanges of speech, deep in the absorption of that complete companionship which needs not speech to express it.

At length the girl arose and said they must go to the house. Her companion hesitated.

"Come up to the house," she said, "and see Eloise and mother. You will stay all night?"

"No," he replied, "not to-night. I don't want to see anybody else to-night. I have to be home early in the morning, and it would be better for the boys not to find me when they come back after midnight."

She acquiesced, with some reluctance. They walked up the lane together, and after a little lingering at the gate, which they had not the heart to deny themselves, he returned to the river, recrossed in the boat, and walked home under the starlight, revolving, along with tender thoughts of her he had left, the growing seriousness of his relations with her daredevil brothers and the rest of the lawless band with whom he was so entangled he could not see the way out.

CHAPTER II.

HISTORICAL AND PERSONAL.

The prince of darkness is a gentleman.
—Shakespeare.

In the early fifties there came to the village of Riverside from a town on the lower Monongahela, in Pennsylvania, one Jacob Holmes, who was a wagon maker, an honest, hard-working man of German stock, past middle age, with half a dozen sons and daughters, of whom two or three were grown to near womanhood and manhood. Holmes was quiet, steady, devoted to his shop, turned out good work, and deserved to prosper.

His eldest son, George, then about coming of age—a good-looking, amiable boy, the pet of an indulgent, injudicious mother—had not been required to enter his father's shop nor to learn any other trade or business. While the father and his journeyman, "Jimmy" English, were driving the shop with unremitting assiduity, George was free to divert himself by riding around visiting relatives, of whom there were several in the neighborhood, or in making other acquaintances and finding means of amusement.

One of the first families to whom he was attracted was the Esmonds, who owned a farm lying along the river on the opposite side from the village, and a short distance below, the homestead being at the lower end of the place, and distinguished by a new owner in later years as "The Great Elm."

In that household were several sons and two daughters, the younger near George's age; and there were usually some hired men about the farm, which seems to have been managed without much system or profit. The elder sons were reputed to be rather wild, and the place was frequented by associates and visitors of kindred description. It was claimed that this younger set had come by their obliquity, their wayward temper and reckless ways, by honest inheritance. A few people believed (but for reasons of prudence did not publish their opinions from the housetops) that darker trades than farming had been carried on about the place from a pretty early day.

Young Holmes found the company he met there suited to his inclinations, and, being of an irresolute temper, with no fixed purpose in life, fond of idleness and pleasure, he by degrees fell entirely under the influence of the stronger spirits with whom he became associated, and was carried along by the current of inclination and circumstances until he became subservient not only to their will and purposes, but imbued with like wild and lawless desires, which drove them from one adventure to another, till there was little too daring or law-defying for them to undertake.

His parents found after a year or two that he was in bad company. They often besought him to give it up, and for the moment he would be penitent and promise to break away from it. But he had gone too far to withdraw, even had he been made of firmer stuff than he was. He had become cognizant of, if not participant in, many of the Esmond gang's offenses, and realized at last that he could not break with them except at the peril of his life. Infirm of purpose, easily swayed by stronger natures, perplexed by the growing distrust of his associates, he shut his eyes to considerations of rectitude or of safety and drifted with the current that was setting strongly towards the cataract.

Harry Esmond—"Handsome Harry"—the elder of the brothers at home, was the leading spirit at this time of a group that embraced more in its fellowship and had wider ramifications than was suspected even by the few in the neighborhood who thought themselves well-informed. He was not by any means the most vicious or desperate of the lot; but he was a natural and recognized leader by virtue of his personal superiority and force of character. He was quick to grasp a situation or see an opportunity, had a cool head and capacity to plan enterprises. He had the generous, large-minded way of dealing with his fellows characteristic of leadership, and they looked to him for direction as naturally as he to them for obedience and support.

"Handsome Harry" never had any liking for work. He might help a little in an emergency like harvest; but the drudgery of regular work or business did not agree with him, and the thought of giving his years to such a humdrum life was not to be entertained. While the paternal Esmond, the younger boys, and the hired men looked after the farm, Harry walked around or rode about like a gentleman of leisure, wore good clothes, kept his hands soft and his brain busy planning means of amusing himself, and, finally, enterprises of greater pith and moment.

Some of his subordinates displayed nature's diplomas on their faces. Lynn Johnson was slight, dark-visaged, hatchet-faced, with snaky black eyes, and had cunning and villainy written in every lineament. Lot Dyson was a great, gaunt, hulking ruffian, with shoulders like Mc-

Ginn's "Irishman" and a face that had the hungry look of a beast of prey, as if some predatory wolf had been reincarnated in his uncouth person. Ray Harris was a big, ox-like, heavy-jawed fellow, rather good-natured on the average, but wholly animal, and controlled by considerations looking to profit or gratification of the grosser kind. In the course of this history this fellow becomes the husband of the elder daughter of the Esmond household, in spite of her repugnance to him, under family pressure. There was an elder son of the Esmond family married and living in the neighborhood, part of the time in the village, without apparent occupation or visible means of support.

At the time this history opens, Harry Esmond had tender relations with the daughter of a blacksmith in the village, one Byers, who lived in an old stone house on the river bank built in Indian times, with walls near a yard thick and windows not much larger than the loopholes in a block-house. This old stone house was for a time quite a resort for the chief of the gang, not always for reasons of gallantry, for the blacksmith seems to have had a pretty intimate knowledge of some of the exploits of Harry and his friends and to have lent a little assistance at times, as occasion seemed to require.

But the village rendezvous of the gang was the Blue Boar tavern, kept by Jonas Blue—among his cronies familiarly "Jone" —who found it profitable to his bar, if not otherwise, to be on good terms with these roystering fellows, who always had money to spend for drink; and he finally appears to have become their confidant, if not coadjutor and adviser, in their lawless exploits.

When Jonas became the owner of the hostelry, he had a big square sign made to be mounted on a post by the pavement, and had the village painter—who, along with his artistic accomplishments, combined, with a pleasant humor, the trades of chairmaker and politician—paint on the panel an enormous black boar, with tusks of almost elephantine length. Through some chemical fault in the paint (possibly) the black, after a few months' exposure to the weather, turned to be "darkly, deeply, beautifully blue." The general opinion of the village was that the transformation was the result of some trick on the part of the waggish painter, but Blue himself saw in it a distinct interposition of Providence in compliment to himself as giving his name to the tavern—and blue the beast was allowed to remain.

While Harry Esmond was inclined and accustomed to plan bold enterprises away from his own neighborhood, some of his followers were not above jobs that could hardly be classed above petty larceny. One night a lot of green hides were stolen from a tannery half a mile south of the village and run off to the country town, where they were sold by Dyson. A little bolder stroke was the robbery of the principal store in the village one Saturday night. An auger was procured by Dyson from the wagon-shop of Jacob Holmes, with which a hole was bored through the shutter and the latch lifted. A small sum of money was taken from the cash drawer and numerous bolts of cloth and cassimere, underclothing, stockings, and other articles of attire were carried away. The merchant and other citizens could guess the direction the goods had gone.

Monday following the robbery Mr. Holmes sent George to haul a load of coal for Lot Dyson, who lived in an old log house on the "hill farm" of the Esmond estate. Lot was to meet him at the foot of the hill where the coal mine was and help him load, but when George arrived Lot was not there, and, loading himself, he drove on up to the house. He went in, and, finding Mrs. Dyson alone, asked for Lot. At this moment; hearing a noise overhead he asked her who was upstairs. She would not tell him, and, being familiar with the house as well as with its inmates, he went upstairs, and, approaching the room from which the noise appeared to come, he pushed against the door (which was insecurely fastened by a wooden button inside). The door flew open and disclosed Dyson, Lynn Johnson, and "Johnny" Hooker, with bolts of goods and clothing spread out on a bed trying to agree on a division. They were surprised by Holmes' appearance, though not disconcerted, for he was in most of their secrets. Hooker, who will be heard of again, wat a natty, well-dressed young fellow from Pennsylvania, who had been visiting for some time at Esmonds', apparently looking for some such job as this. He was an underground agent who assisted them in running off and marketing stolen horses and other property.

A day or two after this, the elder Holmes went with the old ferryman to a neighboring field on the Lot Dyson place to haul a load of fodder, and in tearing down a "shock" they uncovered a bolt of cassimere, which, on being taken to the merchant, was recognized as part of his stolen property. The goods had been concealed temporarily in the cornfield, and this bolt had been overlooked when the spoil had been gathered in for a dividend.

No attempt was made to prosecute the robbers or recover the goods, though evidence and opinion in the village pointed to them directly. They were formidable, and neither the old merchant nor anybody for him felt like making the move. Justice was timid, and the bandits bold and prosperous. A lot of the stolen cassimere was dyed in the Esmond household, and the chief wore a pair of pantaloons of the stuff wrongside-out.

For some years the most profitable adventures of this band were the running off of horses to Pennsylvania. They had a chain of confederates who received the horses, put them in concealment, passing them from one to another at night, till they reached a safe market. Horses fifteen to twenty miles away would disappear some night as mysteriously as if swallowed up by the earth. The trips were planned so that the robbers would reach their hiding-place before daylight. One of their exploits that made a good deal of local excitement was the running off of some fine horses from the farm of Robert Mason, a pioneer on upper Bingamon; another was the robbery of "old Josie" Boyer, on Ten-mile. But nothing ever came of the agitation in either case. Public opinion pointed to the perpetrators, but their tracks were so well covered no tangible proofs could be produced.

The habits and disposition of the country people made the trade of these night riders easy and safe. They went to bed at dark and slept the sleep of the Seven, and if their dogs barked at night at passing horsemen, they gave themselves no concern, so long as their premises were not invaded or their property taken. Men could ride through the country roads at night anywhere on any kind of business with impunity. The people living along the road were far more afraid than they.

CHAPTER III.

THE ALCHEMY OF FIRE.

Fire, faithful servant of the devil.
—Anon.

But sure I think that I can drink
With him that wears a hood.
—Bishop Still.

One of the connections these bandits had at a distance was a burly fellow named Abe Keifer. He operated about Clarksburg and Buckhannon and in the country between. Harry Esmond seemed to keep in close touch with him, and they had frequent meetings to which the public were not invited.

During the period when George Holmes was most completely subservient to Esmond, he and Harry met one night at the Blue Boar. Esmond took him out on the back porch, and, looking cautiously about to be sure no one was within earshot, said:

"I've got a job I want you to help me with, and I don't want the rest to know anything about it."

"I'm your man," said George. "You'll divvy, of course?"

"Yes," replied Harry, "and I'll make it worth your while. I fixed it up with Abe Keifer when I saw him at Elias Tarbert's three weeks ago. You know Abe has a saloon out on the Northwestern road west of Clarksburg. He had it built last winter, and has it insured for double what it cost him. His goods are well insured, and these he will sneak out so as to get the insurance money on them and have the goods besides. Well, the place isn't paying, and he has agreed that if I will tip a match he will divide the profit. I am to have $400 in gold, and if you go with me you shall have half of it."

"Won't I, though!" said George, enthusiastically. "When are we to do it?"

"I just got a letter from Abe this evening. He gave me a key when I saw him, and now he writes me appointing the night it is to be done, and telling me all about it. The letter has lain in the office here several days, and the time fixed is to-morrow night."

"To-morrow night will suit me," quoth George. "I'll ride the black mare."

"And I will get Byers' black horse," said Esmond. "He'll let me have it when I tell what's afoot. I don't want to take a horse from home, because the other boys will want to know where I am going. This dish is 'personal,' and I don't want any of the rest dipping in. They will think I am at Byers' with 'Tot' when we will be on the road that has a pot of gold at the other end."

"I'll go to bed early," said George, in his enthusiasm, "and when the rest are asleep I will slip out and jump on Lize and come around to Byers' for you."

"I will be all ready," said Harry. "Mum's the word."

They separated, and Esmond went to the bar-room, where he found Lot and Ray standing at the bar as if they had just taken a drink.

"Have something, boys, at my expense," said Harry, who felt a little more than ordinarily generous on the strength of that potential $400. "Set her out, Jone."

Blue placed the whisky on the counter, and the invited poured out glasses, Ray three fingers, while Lot filled his to the brim.

Lot noticed the landlord watch him pour out the liquor as if he begrudged so big a drink. "I don't drink no sample," he remarked. "When I drink, I want to taste it."

"That's right, Lot," commented Harry. "There is nothing small about you."

"I was born thirsty," growled Lot, "and I've never been able to get over it."

The landlord, not much pleased with the size of the drinks nor with Harry's encouragement of such lavishness at his expense, interrupted the conversation:

"I hear Jim Munroe says he'll be d——d if he don't make me pay for that horse. Has he been sent off?" he asked, in a lower tone.

"He is under ground all right," said Lot.

Esmond, instead of liquor, had poured out a glass of water, and was sipping it at intervals. Lot observed it, and turned on him: "Why don't you drink something? Water and milk are for children."

"Jone," said Harry, turning to the landlord, "give Lot the bottle and let him drink a glass for me. I don't want anything to-night. I'm going where there's ladies, Lot, and don't want it on my breath," continued Harry, smiling.

Lot poured another brimming glass, to the manifest discomfort of the man behind the bar. "Here's to the ladies and to the chief who breaks their hearts," he said, with a grim sort of politeness and humor, and then he drank off the liquor.

"Thank you," said Harry, as he handed the barkeeper a dollar. "Never mind the change," he said, in a low voice that cleared the landlord's face of the temporary cloud. He in his cheerfulness remarked:

"They say Billy Richardson is raising the whole country about his gray stallion."

"Billy Richardson be d——d," put in

Ray. "When he sees the gray stallion again he'll be older and wiser than he is now."

"What has been done with him?" asked Esmond, looking around cautiously to be sure no outsider had come in.

"Underground with the other," said Lot significantly.

"When is Johnny coming after them?" resumed Harry.

"He is to be here to-morrow night," said Ray. "That stallion will bring $1,000, if he will a dollar, and Johnny will have the money inside a month."

"What am I to do if Jim Monroe sues me?" came back the landlord.

"Oh, he can't make anything out of it," replied Harry. "A landlord can't be made responsible for horses put in his stable by other people without his knowledge. Walker put up that horse without asking your leave. How should you know who took him out, or even that he was there?"

The next night, George spent the evening at home and went to bed with the rest of the family, somewhat to their surprise.

When he thought all asleep, he rose quietly, dressed himself, and went to the stable, saddled and bridled the black mare and led her out by a back way to avoid the possibility of being overheard by the household. A few minutes later he drew up before the stone mansion, where Byers and Harry were standing by the front door. Harry went back to the stable for the horse and in a few minutes joined him, and, waving an adieu to Byers, they set off under the starlight to tempt fortune or fate, as the event might prove.

They rode slowly over the wooden bridge at the border of the village, and a quarter of a mile further on gave rein and relieved their rising spirits with a mile gallop, along which there were then no houses near the road. They had started a little after ten. The distance was a dozen miles. A moderate gait would take them to their destination before one o'clock, and three hours more would bring them back. They moderated speed, but rode in silence. The noise of the horses' hoofs made conversation unsatisfactory in subdued tones, and it was not prudent to talk loud.

When they had arrived within a few hundred feet of the goal of their enterprise, Harry, who had been there more than once and knew the place, dismounted and handed the rein to George, who withdrew beneath the shade of some trees by the roadside.

"Now," he said, "if anything goes wrong, don't run away and leave me."

"Not much!" was the reply.

As he advanced toward the building, Esmond felt in his pocket for the key. It was there, safe enough. He paused a few minutes, looked around him, and listened intently. The saloon stood isolated. There were no inhabited buildings within several hundred yards. The place had been admirably selected for the purpose. Nothing seemed to be stirring in the neighborhood. Keifer in his letter to Esmond had told him where to feel for matches, and where he would find some bottles of brandy and some good cigars. Everything else in the saloon of a portable character had been packed ready to be run off into another part of the country, and the team to take the stuff had waited a short distance away until the vicinity was in bed, and had then gone to the building, loaded the goods, and departed scarcely an hour before the arrival of the incendiaries. The details had been well planned and carefully executed.

Esmond, after another pause of a few moments, listening, and, peering through the dark, unlocked it and entered, closing it softly behind him. He reached out to a shelf beside the door where Keifer had told him to feel for matches, and his hand struck something cold. He recoiled in horror, for it seemed to him for an instant that he had touched a corpse. He held his breath, almost choked with the oppression of indefinite apprehension. No man, however courageous, ever entered a strange house in the dark without an involuntary shudder at the thought of what might be lying in wait for him, for it is the unknown that terrifies, and the unexpected that shocks, as they had just now shocked and terrified Esmond. Visible dangers we instantly summon courage to meet; but the invisible—there is no courage equal to them. Harry stood for a few irresolute moments, and then he remembered that he had matches in his vest pocket, and, taking out one, he struck a match, and with the flash all his apprehensions vanished.

He lit a candle standing near, and, looking around to the shelf, found it was a bottle of brandy that had given him the shock in the dark. He proceeded to take a leisurely survey. Tight shutters, carefully closed, kept the light from showing outside. He found the train that was to be fired. He put the cigars and brandy into portable shape, touched the candle to the tinder, passed out quickly, locking the door after him and throwing the key as far as he could fling it into the field. He walked lightly and swiftly back to the trees where Holmes waited for him with the horses.

"It is all right," he said, in a low voice. "You take these," handing George a part of the packages. He mounted, and they wheeled and rode away in a sudden panic, as if some grim terror were close behind them. At a turn in the road a quarter of a mile distant, they halted and looked back, holding their breath and listening. All was still as death, save the panting of their horses and the throbbing of their own hearts. Evidently there was no alarm. They waited a few minutes, when they saw a light flash up above the saloon, and flames creep out around the eaves. Then, turning, they galloped off toward home, and did not slack speed till they had crossed Limestone and reached a neighborhood where houses were near the road.

When tying up the cigars, Harry had put a handful into his coat pocket. By and by he remembered having done so, and, handing a share of them to Holmes, they lighted and rode along smoking, already in enjoyment of the first fruits of their enterprise. But it may be mentioned here, out of regard for the truth of this history, that no gleam of gold, as the later fruits, ever gladdened George's eyes.

They arrived at the stone mansion just

as the first streamers of the summer dawn were displayed in the eastern sky. Putting their horses in the stable, they found the back door left unfastened, and went up to bed in a room prepared for them and slept until noon.

CHAPTER IV.

ACQUIRING A KENTUCKY TEAM.

There's something in a flying horse.
—Peter Bell.

It was just after harvest time when Esmond got word from their confederate, Tarbert, that a pair of very fine matched Kentucky horses had been brought from Louisville by Tom Boggess, who inherited the fine estate of Ludwell Boggess, consisting of broad and fertile acres, cattle, horses, and lusty negroes. It was a good night's ride to make this trip, and Harry, accompanied by Johnson and Dyson, set out one starlight night to assert their claim to this valuable team.

Tarbert had described to them exactly where the horses would be found and how to approach and get possession of them. The weather being sultry, the horses were tied outside the stable at night to rings in the side of the building, in a small lot approached through bars.

Arrived at the place, Dyson was left in charge of the horses, while Esmond and Johnson went to get the others. After reconnoitering and listening, to be sure the coast was clear, they approached the stable yard and found the horses just as described. They let down the bars softly and went up to the animals, which snorted once or twice with alarm, but, being spoken to soothingly in a low voice, allowed themselves to be untied and led out. As ill-luck would have it, the hindmost, in lifting the last foot over the bars, struck one with a noise that broke sharply on the stillness of the night.

"Who dar?" a moment later came a voice from within the stable. Esmond and Johnson hurried the horses into a trot. The negro, now fully awake, came out of the stable and saw the animals outside the yard and just vanishing in the dark. It did not occur to him at the moment but they had escaped of their own accord. The bars, being often let down at night, did not attract his attention. He started to run after the horses to drive them back, but when he came in full view of them, he saw the men just mounting, and, running forward frantically, he let out a yell which combined all the elements of his astonishment, his fright, and his wish to give the alarm to the house. It was a weird and frightful cry.

At that instant, Dyson, sitting on his horse, just as the others had reached their saddles, raised the cocked pistol he held in his hand and fired full at the negro, not more than five yards distant. That yell was his last. He went down in a heap without a groan.

The two with the led horses took the lead, while Lot fell behind, whip in hand, to prevent lagging, and away the robbers went down the road, the galloping of the horses scarcely heard in the soft dirt highway. But the riders heard, a few moments after they had started, a call from the house to "Sam!" to know what was the matter.

Johnson knew every bridle-path in this neighborhood. "Boys," he said, when they had got a mile or so away, "the road we are now on runs in the direction of Clarksburg. The place we came into it is about a mile ahead. Three miles farther on we strike another road, running north, and I think we had better ride on towards Clarksburg, till we come to that road, which will bring us back into ours at Lumberport. Our pursuers will then think we have gone south, and while we turn north they will ride straight on."

This was accepted as good advice. They rode furiously on the south bound road and saw lights flash up in one or two farmhouses after they had passed, making it certain the pursuers would hear the robbers had gone south. When they reached the north and south road they turned into it and rode at least two miles before they passed a house within hearing. After this they felt so confident of their safety that they slowed down and let the horses blow. The Kentuckies were fine travelers, and had scarcely turned a hair, rapid as the pace had been.

"Lot," said Johnson, when they had come down to a speed that admitted of talk, "that was a daisy shot of yours. The fellow went down like an ox—never whimpered."

"By ——, it just takes me!" said Lot, with unconcealed pride. "Teach the d——d nigger how to yell at his betters."

A complete account of the Boggess end of the story was furnished by Tarbert on a visit to Esmond's not long after the event. Great was the rage and excitement when it was found Tom's famous bays were gone, and that his stable-boy had been shot. Here was the value of a negro, not less than $1,500, added to the $1,500 Tom had paid for the horses in Louisville, to say nothing of freight and other expenses. But, strange to relate, in the course of a half-hour the poor fellow, who was supposed to be dead, showed signs of life, and in a few minutes more sat up and wanted to know what was the matter.

"Matter!" roared Tom; "you've been killed."

"Guess not, Mars Tom. But did you get the horses?"

When called on from the house for the cause of the alarm, the negro was not in a condition to tell, and it took the people in the house some time to get their wits together and find out what had happened. It took still longer to organize pursuit. The other farm horses were in the pasture, and it took some time to catch and saddle them. It was risky for one or two men to pursue a gang who were evidently strong enough and well-armed enough to make pursuit dangerous. Then pistols had to be hunted up and got in shape, for people in that peaceful neighborhood were not accustomed to keep an armory for service under their pillows.

It was a couple of hours before the pursuers took the road, and they went straight towards Clarksburg, just as Johnson had suggested, while the bays were galloping away towards the opposite point of the compass. The horses had been brought by train to Clarksburg and there unloaded, had been seen by a good many people, and had excited their admiration—possibly the cupidity of some. Naturally, Tom Boggess looked in that direction for the robbers. Search was vigorously prosecuted in that quarter and kept up for a long time. But the owner never saw or heard of his horses again, and, like Rachel weeping for her children, he would not be comforted.

The robbers reached cover before day, and it may be added, to complete the history of the adventure, that the horses went through by the underground route, and were sold in Pittsburg to a rich railroad man for $2,000, and were considered a bargain. After the underground charges had all been paid, $1,500 remained to be divided among Esmond and his retainers, the Chief, as usual, receiving the lion's share.

It appeared from Tarbert's report that when the blood had been washed off the negro's head, it was found that Dyson's bullet had only cut the skin and glanced off the skull. It had knocked the poor fellow instantly insensible, but had done no serious or permanent injury. When Lot Dyson heard this part of the report—that the negro was not killed, after all, by his crack shot—he was unutterably disgusted. "D——n a nigger, anyhow!" he said. "You can't even kill one."

CHAPTER V.

A WATER HAUL.

Oh, my prophetic soul.. Mine Uncle.
—Shakespeare.

The nearest neighbor to the Esmonds, on a farm lying just back of theirs, was Joseph Diedrich (colloquially, "Old Jo" Diedrich), a man of Falstaffian figure, who handled a good deal of live stock, particularly hogs, and who, along with his avoirdupois, had acquired considerable solid wealth. He understood very well the character of his river neighbors, and realized that he must live at peace with them, if at all. He shut his eyes to their offenses, of which he knew a great deal more than he wished, and they, as if by a tacit understanding, let the old man carefully alone.

But even the longest forbearance has its limits. "I don't see," remarked Johnson, one Sunday, when four of the gang were under the big elm, two sitting on the rough bench, whittling its edges, as usual, and the others standing or walking around in the shade, "why Uncle Jo shouldn't divide with us some of his superfluous wealth. Do you know what he did? He rode up the lane the other night, just after dark, carrying in his hand, just tied up loose in a pocket handkerchief, $1,000 in gold and silver."

"The d——l!" said Lot. "What does he take us for—angels? I wonder."

"And," resumed Johnson, "it could have been snatched out of his hand, or he could have been tumbled off his horse, just as easy! Now," he went on, "I want to tell you something I have found out. It don't make any difference how I got it. Old Jo is going to Clarksburg next Wednesday to get money out of the bank to pay Pete Righter for that Laurel Run farm. The first payment is $3,500, and he is to take it over to Righter's the next morning. Now, why should we allow that money to pass through our domain without paying duty? I don't believe in permitting money to be exported from our jurisdiction at all.

The balance of trade ought to be in our favor. Instead of exporting money, we ought to confiscate it."

"That's what I say," chimed in Lot. "If we are going to let all the money be carried out of the neighborhood by the bloated aristocracy, what's going to be left for honest citizens to live on?"

"Boys," observed Harry. "You two ought to be sent to Congress for your masterly views on political economy."

"What's p'lit'cal 'con'my?" asked Lot.

"The science of trover and conversion," replied Harry.

"Worse and worse," groaned Lot.

"But, I tell you," resumed Esmond, "I don't like to lay a tax on Uncle Jo. He is a little 'bloated' in his person, it is true, but he is not an aristocrat. He is our near neighbor, and we ought to try to live on good terms with our neighbors, especially when they know as much about us as he does. He has always treated us white."

"Do you call it 'white,'" growled Lot, "to carry money round in a hankecher, like it was tea or coffee he had been buyin' at the store, just to fool honest people, or to lead 'em into temptation? I call it wrong and unchristian. It's a violation of the Lord's prayer."

The spectacle of such a creature setting himself up as the guardian of the Lord's prayer was too much for the gravity of the others, and Lot was laughed out of countenance.

"All the same," resumed Johnson, "the times are getting pretty hard again, and it is time we collected another installment from somebody. If anybody else will come along to grease the wheels, why, let old Jo go; but if they won't, and he puts himself in our way as a temptation, it will not be our blame if our virtue should be overcome."

"I don't know which most to admire in you, Johnson—the statesman, the financier, or the Christian philosopher," observed Harry.

"Well, I'm talking sense, anyhow; I'll leave it to Lot."

"Your head is level," quoth the sententious Dyson.

"When do you say it is, Johnson?" asked Esmond.

"He will come down from Clarksburg with the money next Wednesday evening, and if we don't have that money to pay for the drinks at the Blue Boar at midnight Wednesday night, it will be our fault, and not the fault of Providence, which offers us the chance. I don't think there is a soul outside of the old man's family that knows anything about this except me," persisted Lynn. It was hard for him to let go such an opportunity. "Uncle Jo never goes to Clarksburg but he has a good deal of business, and he always winds up the day by taking a little more 'booze' than is good for him. He will be late getting away, and he won't reach home till long after dark. It will be dark when he strikes the Maulsby bridge. If he was called on for cash away up there, neither he nor anybody else would ever lay it to anyone in this quarter."

"But suppose he comes home earlier?" queried Harry.

"Then," replied Johnson, "we would give that up, and lay for him next morning on the road to Righter's. You see," continued Johnson, with growing enthusiasm, "we could follow the river road around by Jim Denham's and arrive in the woods near the bridge, the chances are, without being seen by a soul along the road."

"But the old man might know us," suggested Harry. "We would have to wear masks, and he might know our voices; or he might recognize us by our size or shape. He would know Lot by his shoulders. There is not such another pair in the county."

"Chances are," remarked Lot, "he'll be too boozy to know us from a side of sole leather."

"Chances are," rejoined Harry, "he won't be boozy at all, for if he is going to carry that much money he'll keep sober so as to take care of it. Old Jo is no fool. Boys, it is too risky. If it was anybody else—any stranger—it might do."

Esmond left them and walked up to the house. The others whittled a little while in silence, turning over the words of the chief.

"I tell you what, boys," Johnson began, "don't you think we might do a little business on our own account? If we get the swag, we'll divide with Harry. If we don't—and I don't see that—we'll say nothing about it, and pick our flints for another time."

"We ought to do it," said Dyson, decidedly. "I haven't had any drink money for a week without asking Harry for it."

Harris hesitated. He felt undecided; he did not like to act against the chief's advice.

"The way to do," said Johnson, "would be for us to meet at a certain hour near the bridge. I will go up to Sardis to see Tarbert, who ought to have something on the string for us by this time, and I will come around by Lyons'. You two can come by the river road, or one each way, as you please."

"I am agreed," said Ray, finally. "The place to do it will be in the bridge, which is covered, you know, and will be the darkest place."

Nothing more was said to Esmond, who supposed the scheme was abandoned. The three made the necessary excuses to account for their absence, and met at the concerted hour and place. They hid in the woods a couple of hours before dark, and one of them posted himself where he could see all who passed along the road. Darkness fell, and yet their stout old friend had not made his appearance.

"I told you so," said Johnson, when they had got together again. "He'll be late and boozy, just as I said."

"And lousy with gold eagles," added Lot.

Twice did horsemen pass down the road to the bridge, but each time the figure of the rider disappointed the expectation of the watchers. The old man was excessively obese—literally as broad as long, and his figure on horseback was unmistakable—indeed, almost comical. Another horse's hoofs resounded on the hard road and this time they saw a horse on the way carrying something that looked in the dusk like an enormous wool-sack on end. They slipped on to the bridge and retreated to the darkness of the middle. The horse as it advanced showed signs of fright, but came on under the urging of the rider. Suddenly Dyson sprang out, seized the bridle and jerked the animal back almost on its haunches, nearly upsetting the rider.

"For God's sake, gentlemen!" cried the old man, "don't kill me. What do you want?"

"Your money!" replied a hoarse voice, like the snarl of a wolf.

"You're welcome to all I have," said the victim, "though it is not worth taking." He handed over his pocketbook, saying he thought there was about $4 in it.

"We want the money you got from the bank."

"From the bank!" echoed the old man, blankly.

"Yes, and be quick about it."

"I got no money from the bank."

"D——n you, hand out that roll quick," growled the wolf, more menacingly.

"For heaven's sake," pleaded the aged victim, "if you don't believe me, search me."

"Get down, then."

Jo Diedrich descended, not without difficulty, and the bridge trembled with the impact when he struck it. He stood like a lamb waiting to be shorn. The ruffians thrust quick hands into all his pockets and felt all over him for a roll or coin concealed under his clothes, but the net result of the search, in addition to the pocketbook they already had, was: A plug of tobacco, a jack-knife, and a small bottle of whisky. The latter Lot appropriated without remark.

"Gentlemen," said Mr. Diedrich, gently and politely, "there has been some mistake, but it is not my fault. I was at the bank to-day, and did expect to bring some money home with me to pay to Peter Righter; but he happened to be in Clarksburg. We met at the hotel and went to the bank together, and the money was passed to his credit. I am sorry to disappoint you."

"Then take your d——d old pocketbook and go on."

The highwaymen restored also the knife and tobacco. Lot forgot about the whisky. They had scarcely got off the bridge before their ears caught the sound of approaching horses' feet.

"Might have been worse if we had stayed a little longer," remarked Ray.

The poor old victim felt around in the dark till he found his hat, which had fallen off when the horse recoiled, and, leading the animal to the end of the bridge and to a fence near by, he managed, with the vantage thus afforded, to remount. At this moment the rider whose approach had alarmed the robbers came out of the bridge and asked Mr. Diedrich what was the matter. He replied that his horse had got scared in the bridge and he had lost his hat and had to get down for it.

An hour later he drew up at the Blue Boar and asked for the landlord.

"Why, Uncle Jo! is this you?"

"Yes, Blue. Bring me a big drink of whisky. I'm not feeling well."

As he pulled out his pocketbook to pay, the landlord holding up the lantern to enable him to see, the old man quietly remarked:

"I was pretty near losing the $4 in this pocketbook an hour ago."

"How was that?"

"I was held up by three robbers in the Maulsby bridge."

"The dickens!" ejaculated Blue. "How did you get away?"

"I didn't get away. They got away—with me!" The old man gurgled a little laugh at his joke. The liquor made him feel more cheerful. "They thought I had a big lot of money that I was to pay Pete Righter. But Righter met me at the bank and the money was paid over there. They were so disgusted they gave me back my pocketbook, my knife, and my tobacco, but they forgot to give me back my bottle of whisky, else I wouldn't have had to call you out."

"You are lucky to get off so well. Did you know the robbers?"

"Not from Adam. It must have been somebody from Clarksburg who found out I was going to draw the money."

But as he rode away he said to himself:

"Just the same, I know the fellows like a book. I have seen them too often not to know every one of them the darkest night that ever blowed. But if they will let me alone, I'll let them alone. But I wonder how they found out about the money?"

CHAPTER VI.

SETTLING THE SCORE.

No more of that, Hal, an' thou lovest me..
—Shakespeare.

Half an hour after the landlord's interview with Uncle Jo, Harry Esmond came into the Blue Boar.

"I've great news to tell you," was Blue's first greeting.

"Out with it, then," returned Harry, with a momentary tremor, lest it might be something alarming—for conscience does make cowards of us all.

"Old Jo Diedrich was robbed at the Maulsby bridge not two hours ago."

"You don't say!" exclaimed Harry, in blank astonishment.

"Yes. He stopped here about half an hour ago and called me out to give him a drink, and told me all about it. He was set on in the bridge by three men, who told him they wanted a big lot of money he had drawn out of the bank. He gave them his pocketbook with $4 in it, and they searched him, but all they got was his knife, tobacco, and a small bottle of whisky. When they found he didn't have the money they were so disgusted, he says, that they gave him back everything except the whisky."

This was a flood of illumination for Harry. He recalled the talk Sunday under the big elm. Despite his dissent, the others had undertaken the job, and made a fiasco of it.

"Jone," he said, "this is the raciest of the season. I can tell you all about it"—and he did.

"Do you think Uncle Jo knew the boys?" he asked Blue.

"He said he didn't know them from Adam."

"We'll tell them," said Harry, "that he recognized them. It's safe to bet they will be here before midnight after a drink to blunt the edge of their disappointment, and I want to be here when they come. We'll have a little fun with them. I'm going out calling, and will be back. Don't shut up."

Harry Esmond returned to the Blue Boar between eleven and twelve, and, true enough, found the three worthies lounging in the chairs in the bar-room. They looked out of sorts, and were evidently surprised to see him. "Lynn," he said, "what did Tarbert have to say? Has he any business for us?"

"He didn't know a thing," replied Johnson, "except that there is going to be races at Sardis two weeks from Saturday."

"Where were you this afternoon?" turning to Harris.

"Oh, I went over to Bingamon. I had a little business with an uncle of mine. He was owin' me some money, and I thought he might be ready to pay."

"How much was he owing you?" asked Harry. "As much as $3,500?"

"Not so much as that," replied Ray, a trifle surprised. "I wish somebody did owe me that much."

"Did you get the money?" persisted Harry.

"Not a d——n cent."

"These uncles are mighty poor pay," observed Harry. "Which one of your uncles was it?" he kept on. "Was it your 'Uncle Jo'?"

"I ain't got no Uncle Jo," replied Harris, a little sullenly.

"Have any of the rest of you been to see your uncle?"—looking around at the others, who did not even smile in reply.

"Boys," said Esmond, "we are on to you fellows to-night. Uncle Jo Diedrich stopped here about half-past nine o'clock and called 'Jone' out to give him a drink, and told him all about it. He knows every mother's son of you, and is furious."

"Good God!" broke from the astounded Harris, while Dyson and Johnson gave voice to explosives equally profane and expressive of astonishment and dismay. They sat for a moment staring at Esmond with wide-open eyes and mouth. He was enjoying the situation to the top of his bent. "Yes," he went on, "old Jo swears you scared him out o. r year's growth, and that Dyson swore all the hair off his head."

"Nobody could ever do that," interrupted Dyson. (Uncle Jo was bald as a billiard ball.)

"More than that," resumed Harry, "he says he has registered an oath that unless he gets that bottle of whisky back inside of twenty-four hours by the watch, he will have every one of you in the jug before Saturday night."

"Do you think old Jo really knew us?" asked Johnson, turning to the landlord, who nodded an affirmative.

"Knew you!" said Harry. "He knew you all as well as he knows his own children. Why shouldn't he? I told you he would.

"You remember our talk Sunday, Lynn," Esmond resumed. "You said if you didn't have old Jo's money to pay for the drinks at the Blue Boar at midnight to-night, it would be your fault, and not the fault of Providence. I'm waiting for you to set them up. That's what I came in for. It lacks five minutes of midnight, it is true" (looking at his watch), "and I can wait for time. But if you don't have the money then, we have got to have the drinks anyhow, and you will have to settle with Providence, which shall be responsible to 'Jone' for the score—unless Lot, there," he went on, turning to Dyson, who sat in gloomy silence, "will bring out that bottle of Uncle Jo's."

"Say, now, Harry," begged Lot, "don't be hard on us. That bottle is as dry as—as I am."

Harry smiled at the force of the simile. "Then you had better have it filled with good whisky and send it to Uncle Jo before to-morrow night."

"I'll set up the drinks, boys, if I have credit enough," put in Johnson; "but I don't believe there is enough cash among us three to pay for washing the glasses."

"By the way, Lynn," said Harry, as if it had just occured to him, "perhaps you would not mind telling us now, just in confidence, how you found out Uncle Jo was going to bring that money home with him. Getting information is a great art, especially in our trade."

"That is a family secret," replied Lynn, "which I do not feel at liberty to disclose."

"I suppose you have no objection to disclosing your present views on tariffs, exports, and confiscation? Did the old man lead you into temptation, Lot, with that bottle of whisky? That sort of thing ought to be forbidden in the by-laws, for the protection of 'honest citizens.' Men ought not to be allowed to run at large on the highways with bottles of whisky in their pockets—or was he carrying it 'loose in his handkerchief'? It is against public policy and the Lord's prayer. It's what I call 'unchristian.'"

"Now, Harry," said Lot, "don't kick a feller when he's down."

"Boys," said the chief, loftily, looking them over as if they had been children, "I ought to let you go home to-night without a drop. It would teach you a lesson you need. But I am not quite cruel enough for that. Set out the bottle, 'Jone,' with the big glasses. And I think we had better have something to eat. There's nothing makes a fellow so hungry as missing a little morsel of about $3,500 in gold."

As the others filled their glasses in the generous fashion common to them, Harry poured out a glass of water, and, lifting it toward his lips as they raised theirs, said:

"Lads, I want to offer you a sentiment that you may take home and think of in your beds: Here's to the three knights of the road who took pity on the sorrows of a poor old man and gave him back everything except what he needed most—his bottle of whisky. When you go prospecting for gold again, may you never strike so lean a 'pocket' nor capture so small a bottle."

All laughed as they drank off their liquor, and then Harry bade them fill again. They fell to with the appetite of threshing machines, and when they finally started for home there was not a crumb left for the mice, and the barkeeper's bottle was as dry as Uncle Jo Diedrich's.

CHAPTER VII.

DECOYING GAME.

Bloody instructions, which, being taught,
Return to plague the inventor.
—Shakespeare.

One evening near the last of May, a little after sundown, Harry Esmond rode up to the Blue Boar, and, throwing the rein over the hitching-post, walked through to the back porch. The landlord's wife was a few feet away in the garden dropping some seeds in a flower bed that had been prepared by the hired man during the day. Hearing the step on the porch, she looked up and came towards him.

"Where is 'Jone'?" he asked.

"He was here a minute ago," she said. "Come in, and I will see if I can find him.

"You look as if you had something on your mind," she said, as they walked into the hall. "How is 'Tot'?" she asked, smiling mischievously.

"She was well when I last saw her"—with a shade of embarrassment.

"When is it to come off?"

"You'll have to ask her. How should I know?"

"Now, Harry, you know it does not rest with Tot. She worships the ground you walk on."

"Why," he said, pleased at the flattery, but trying to hide it, "I'm a little afraid of the old lady. I'm afraid Maria doesn't approve of me."

"Nonsense!" she replied; "you know better; Maria is your best friend."

"Oh, well," said Harry, wishing to dismiss the subject, "we'll have to wait till I make a strike."

At this moment the landlord entered the hall from the street, and, seeing Esmond and his wife in conversation, came forward smilingly, with an inquiring look at Harry.

"Jone, I want to see you," the latter said, turning with an apologetic bow to the wife.

"Some fresh mischief afoot!" she threw back gayly, as she walked away.

"Come into the back room," said the landlord, leading the way to a little den off to one side of the bar-room where he was accustomed to receive friends who had matters to talk over that were not for publication.

"What is it?" he asked, perceiving, as his wife had, that Esmond had "something on his mind."

"It's a peach," said the latter.

"This is not the time of year for peaches," quoth the other.

"Well, it is game, then. Game is always in season with us, you know."

"Tell me about it," said Jonas, eagerly.

Esmond stepped to the door, looked out, to be sure no one was within hearing, and, shutting it softly, came back and sat down again.

"I got word last night," he said, "that a rich grazier from Fayette County was coming up into this neighborhood to buy some cattle. He wants two or three hundred yearlings and two-year-olds to graze on a big grass farm he has on the slopes of Laurel Hill. Our friends managed to get his ear and have filled him up with a story that he can find what he is looking for in this neighborhood. He ought to be here now inside of a week. He makes a trip of this kind every year, and carries money with him in a belt to pay for his purchases, paying half on closing a deal, and the other half when the cattle are delivered on his farm. Our friends think he ought to have $3,000 or $4,000 in his belt."

"He won't have that much when we get through with him," remarked the other. "But, now, what is your plan?"

"That is what I want to talk with you about. He inquired about hotels, and was advised to put up at the Blue Boar. He will probably arrive in the evening. You will know him, even if he should not tell his business. He rides a very stylish bay horse and will be dressed in ordinary farmers' jeans. He is a man about fifty, wears gray side whiskers, and has a big nose. As soon as you can get at him you can sound him. He will probably tell you his object, and you are then to tell him that you know just where he can find what he is looking for, and you think he can get a bargain. Send him to the big elm. It is better none of us should be here to go with him. You can direct him how to find the place, and try to have him come before he makes inquiries in any other part of the neighborhood. We will be on the lookout for him, and if he comes our boys will see that he is well taken care of."

"This is as straight as a string," said Blue, with animation. "I will try to get him away before anybody else finds out his business or knows where he is going. Then there will be no questions asked."

The conversation had been carried on in very low tones. After a brief silence, Blue asked: "Is George working for you now?"

"No—and he has not been down for a week or two."

"I think," resumed the landlord, "it will be better for him not to know anything about this. He has not got the nerve for a job of this kind, and I'm afraid he can't hold his tongue."

"You're right," rejoined the other. "I'm afraid George is weakening, and it will not do to let him know too much."

A light step approached the door, and the voice of the landlord's wife was heard: "Jone, you are wanted in the bar."

Esmond rose. "I am going around to Byers' for a while, and may come back after a little, but don't sit up for me. But if I don't come back, and should not see you before the belt arrives, send me word right away."

Before he reached the sidewalk, Esmond had changed his mind about the visit to the stone mansion. The bantering of the landlord's wife had awakened some unpleasant thoughts regarding his relations with the blacksmith's daughter. Marriage with her was something he had not thought of. It was evident the village gossip was connecting their names in a way to suggest this, and he must be more discreet. He unhitched his horse, and, mounting, rode towards home. "When I have made my pile," ran his secret thoughts as he rode along, "I will pull out from this neighborhood and begin life anew somewhere else. Some day this place will get too hot for me."

CHAPTER VIII.

TRAPPED.

He shall return no more to his house, neither shall his place know him any more.—Bible.

It was two weeks later when a stranger rode into the village by the Fairmont road just at dusk, and, continuing along the street till he saw the sign at the corner, drew rein at the Blue Boar and dismounted. A man was standing at the corner who looked as if he might be connected with the house, and the stranger asked him if he was. It happened to be Guy Esmond, who replied that he would call the landlord, and asked him to walk into the public room. In a few minutes mine host entered and met the stranger with complaisant and hospitable air.

"I want to stay over night," said the man.

"Supper, of course?"

"Yes; I have been riding all day, and am sharp set."

The guest was shown to a room, and, having refreshed himself with a basin of water and a clean towel, was conducted to the supper room. The horse was put away, and the landlord clearly recognized in both man and beast the "game" that had been scented a fortnight before. Although it had not appeared when expected, there could be no mistaking the description.

The landlord went to the supper room, and, assisting to supply the wants of his guest, sought to engage him in conversation. For a time he was too busy for words, but after his hunger had been somewhat appeased, he was disposed to talk. He said he had come to this neighborhood to look for some young cattle. He had been advised to come to this place, and could the landlord tell him where he might find what he was looking for?

Mine host, with an engaging air of interest and sincerity, replied that within a few days he had heard of a fine lot of yearlings that were to be sold because the owner, not being able to renew some farm leases that had about expired, would not have pasturage for the cattle this season. He thought it likely they might be bought at a bargain by anyone who would take the round lot.

The stranger showed marked interest in the information, and, on learning that the cattle were at a place no more than a mile distant, said he would go there the first thing after breakfast, when he would ask the landlord to direct him. Meanwhile, as he was very tired, he would go to bed, and was directly shown to his room.

Blue had dropped a hint to Guy not to go away till he could see him; so the latter lingered about the door till the stranger had retired.

"Come with me," said Blue, passing out to the pavement and turning down the street towards the stable. "I can't take time now," he said, "to explain to you who this man is, but it is somebody Harry has been expecting, and I was to send him word as soon as the man arrived. Harry will tell you all about it, and he may want your help."

He went to the stable, took one of his horses out of the stall, saddled and bridled it, and, leading it to the door, said: "Now you jump on and ride down to old Nickie's and tell Harry the man he was expecting from Fayette County is here, and will go over to see the cattle the first thing in the morning. He will understand."

"Oh!" gasped Guy, opening his eyes in surprise, and comprehending that something was afoot.

"You tell Harry just what I said, and don't lose any time."

At a late hour the horse was brought back by one of the chief's younger brothers.

Next morning the cattle buyer was up early. He was ready for an early breakfast, which was ready for him. No time had been lost. The landlord pointed out to him the direction he was to go, and described roads and destination so he could not miss his way, and the man paid his reckoning and rode off towards the river, scarcely noticed, if seen at all, by anybody in the village.

CHAPTER IX.

A WILD ROSE.

The gods have made only two perfect things: a woman and a rose.—Anon.

Loraine Esmond was like the wild rose that lifts the tender grace of its beauty in the midst of noxious growths, assimilating, through the divine chemistry of nature, only the elements required to nurture its delicate loveliness from the same soil that supplies the grosser essences to the rank ragwort and the pestilent thistle.

She had been born into an environment of grossness and criminality, but the stain of her surroundings had never touched her. From the time she came to have her first perception of associations and surroundings, she had been repulsed and distressed by them. Her mother had never had any patience with the scruples, the questionings, the "pride"—as she chose to consider it—which set the girl apart from the rest as belonging to a different sphere. The fathers and brothers had been fond of her and petted her when she was a child, but never for a moment had they entered into her deeper life nor sympathized in any degree with her finer nature, which they were incapable of comprehending; nor had they ever caught the faintest glimpse of the point of view from which she regarded their actions and motives, to which they gave themselves unreservedly, without question or doubt.

She was a stray in that flock—a reincarnation, by a freak of heredity, of some finer and statelier soul that had dignified the family tree before the devil came into later possession. Her clearer eye saw, in its true colors and with profound horror, the moral obliquity of those bound to her by the closest ties of nature, and never since she had arrived at the age of this perception, had she been without an oppressive sense of impending evil or danger.

Her elder sister, while kind and affectionate with her, had never been able to enter into her feelings or to see the things she saw so clearly. She lacked the younger girl's delicacy of soul, her intuitive recognition of the line between right and wrong, grossness and refinement, and considered her foolish and impracticable. She herself would have been glad if their life had been different, for there was much that grated upon her womanly nature; glad if the male members of the household had been more tractable and more conformable to the usages of the society around them, plain and simple as it was. But she was not shocked nor distressed by their conduct, and did not feel that she had any right to question what they did. She had that submissiveness characteristic of the domestic animals to the domination of stronger wills, and to what appeared to be the inevitable. Yet when Ray Harris, the hired man, let her see that he was an admirer—and finally became a suitor for her favor—nature revolted and she repulsed him, time after time, with natural scorn. But as he, more and more strongly entrenched in his hold on the family through knowledge of their fatal secrets, persisted in his suit, she, understanding the strength of his position, and admonished, first by the demeanor of her brothers, and at last by the words of her mother, that his suit dare not be denied, began to realize the impossibility of resistance, like the bird in the forest when it feels the spell of the first ray from the glittering eye of the rattlesnake. As time passed, the coil was drawn tighter and tighter around the helpless girl, and, yielding at last, because she was powerless to resist, she accepted her fate stolidly, as the beast of burden accepts the halter, and became Ray Harris' wife. It was a quiet wedding, for all were conscious that it was a shameful one, and there was nothing to be happy over or proud of. The sacrifice had been consummated despite all the tears and protests of Loraine, who could find no words to express her horror and detestation of the outrage.

Loraine herself had not lacked for suitors. Many of the young fellows who came about the place had sought her smiles; but she was separated from them by an infinite space which they had no conception of nor she any power to cross. George Holmes had touched her compassion because she perceived that while weak he was not depraved; that there was a core of virtue in the boy that needed only good influences and exemption from evil to shape his life into a worthy manhood; and this compassion, through the necessity of her nature to find something to love, had ripened into affection. She was so much his superior in strength, as in fineness of soul, that her love had in it an unconscious maternity of anxiety for his reformation and welfare. By every means in her power she had sought to fortify him against the influences that surrounded her and which he could not visit her without encountering. Had he been strong enough to go away from the neighborhood and begin a new course of life elsewhere, to stay away till he was thoroughly weaned from these evil influences, till he had made a beginning in the world and developed self-reliance and character—as she had over and over again advised—she could see, and had tried to get him to see, that there might be a future for them; for then not interposing seas or mountains, time or space, could have kept her from sharing his life. But he was like the silly moth that worships the flame. He could not keep away from her, much less go away where he could not see her. The thought of such an even temporary separation was insupportable. Nor could he visit the Esmond home without wishing to be on good terms with the rough brothers who dominated it.

The girl's influence drawing her lover away from that of her brothers and their lawless associates, made him reluctant and lukewarm about seconding them in their adventures. They were quick to perceive this feeling and attributed it to any reason but the right one. They began to distrust him; and when some things that he in his penitent hours had confided to his father, who in turn had confided them to a relative, began to leak and come to the ears of the band, they taxed George openly with treachery. He denied it indignantly and tried to restore himself to their confidence by redoubled zeal in their plans and enterprises. But confidence is a tender plant, and one breath of distrust is fatal to it. He himself felt the chill of this breath whenever he visited the Esmond home; and as he kept nothing from Loraine that was of mutual concern, she, too, shared his apprehensions and suffered far more keenly from the growing perils than he. For his part, so long as he could bask in the light of her eyes, nothing could give him much real anxiety. Nothing like honor, manhood, ambition, weighed in the scale—such was his infatuation—poor, weak, happy, temporizing fool!

CHAPTER X.

A DIVIDEND.

He will give the devil his due.
—Shakespeare.

It was a week after the cattle-buyer had been at the Blue Boar before Harry Esmond visited the village. Guy had been at the tavern two or three times; but in answer to the landlord's hints of inquiry, he had maintained a discreet silence, only saying matters were "all right" and that Harry was coming up in a day or two. Harry walked over and, true to his owlish instincts, came into the village after dark.

He was playing a deep game with his friend of the Blue Boar. The booty had exceeded their expectations. A large part of the money was in gold, which could be used anywhere without risk. The rest was in notes of two Wheeling banks—the Northwestern Virginia and the Merchants' and Manufacturers'. It will be remembered that at this period the currency was made up of local or state banks, and money that was current in one place might be uncurrent or subject to a heavy discount in another a few hundred miles away. It was necessary for a business man who expected to use money to procure notes that would be current where he would need to use them. The Esmonds had agreed among themselves that they would not give up any more of this booty than absolutely necessary to secure their safety. The connections in Pennsylvania would have to have a good share, for safety and future business depended on satisfying them; but the publican of the Blue Boar must not expect too much for his subordinate part as decoy. He had done nothing but send the man to his death. They who did the work were entitled to the lion's share. Thus argued the chief, who held the strings of the bag.

He entered the Blue Boar by the side door and, walking back on the porch, looked in at the rear door of the bar-room. The landlord behind the bar saw him, though none of the loungers did, and excusing himself to them for a few minutes locked the bar and came out to the back room where Harry was waiting for him. He closed the door, struck a match and lit a candle.

"Well?" he said, turning to Esmond with an interrogation point in the word and in his face.

"Well," replied the latter, "it is all right, but it was not as big game as we thought it would be. The old fellow didn't have any belt, and he had only about $1,200 on him. A part of this was in gold, which he carried in an inside pocket of his underclothes."

Blue sat for a full half minute without a word, disappointment in every line of his saturnine face. "Is that so?" he said, at last, in unaffected disgust. He saw his share of the spoil dwindling to small proportions and realized that he would have to modify some plans he had been constructing in the air during the past few days.

"Johnny and the others down below," resumed Esmond, "claim half; and when they find out how little that is, they will be awfully disappointed and hard to satisfy. And we have got to satisfy them somehow, as you know."

"Honor bright," said Blue, "is that the way it pans out?"

"Honor bright," returned the other, without the quiver of a nerve. "You know I wouldn't go back on you in a matter of this kind."

The landlord gave a long, low whistle, as if with the expulsion of his breath he was getting rid of his chagrin.

"I have brought you a hundred dollars of the gold," said Esmond. "I thought you would rather have that than the notes. It is safer to handle, for notes might be marked. After we have settled with the people down below, if we can make a good settlement may be I can squeeze you out fifty dollars more, but don't count on it."

As he spoke he drew from his pocket a small packet. "There's ten gold eagles. I wish it was a thousand."

"And so do I," said the greedy Jonas as he undid the paper and caught the yellow gleam of the money. His eyes were not above sparkling for such an insignificant sum as even ten eagles, and he bestowed them safely in his pocket. "A hundred dollars," he said, after a little pause, "is not to be despised, but it is not enough for the risk."

"That is one of the risks we have to take," remarked Harry. "We may get something; we may get nothing. But whichever it is, we have to put up with it. Better luck next time. It was neatly done, and I don't think there will ever be any trouble."

The landlord would have liked to know the particulars of the job; but somehow both felt it an unpleasant thing to talk about. "What about the horse?" he asked.

"We don't dare run him down the river. He might be recognized and traced. He is in under ground now, and tomorrow night Lot or Ray will take him up to Tarbert, who will send him on to Abe. He can be marketed in that quarter without risk."

CHAPTER XI.

GATHERING CLOUDS.

Be thou faithful unto death.—Bible.

The Sunday after the cattle-buyer had been at the Blue Boar, young Holmes went down to Esmond's. He planned his visit for an hour when he knew Loraine would be freed from household duties, and he asked her to walk with him to the river. The path beside the river road was the favorite ramble. It was shaded, secluded, beautiful in its wealth of leafage and in the presence of the glistening river. They walked down the river, in preference to up, for a reason neither could have put into words, because a few hundred feet brought them to the limit of the Esmond farm; and when they had passed that they always seemed to be treading a freer and happier soil. The place had grown for each a grievous presence that they were glad, even for an hour, to be free from.

At the end of a half mile they came to a great sycamore whose curving roots offered them seats, and here they sat down to enjoy the peaceful seclusion. They had talked of ordinary matters on the way, and now they sat a little while in silence. George spoke first: "Father mentioned at the house that he saw a stranger coming down this way early the other morning and he wondered if it was somebody going to your house. Father had been to mill before breakfast and saw the man get off the ferryboat and turn down this way. He noticed the stranger was riding a very handsome horse."

Loraine's face paled as if with a painful emotion. She hesitated and her lover noticed the internal struggle and looked at her inquiringly.

"Yes, George, there was a stranger at our house early Friday morning. He came to buy cattle. He said he had been told by the landlord at the Blue Boar tavern that we had a fine herd of yearlings and would sell them because, having given up some farms we had under lease, we would not have pasture for them."

George looked his surprise. She resumed:

"You know we have no cattle to sell; but Ray and Guy told him they would go with him up to the hill farm past Lot's and show him the cattle."

Speech failed the girl, and it seemed as if she would choke in an agony of feeling. But presently having mastered the emotion, she went on:

"The stranger did not come back with them; and I suppose he went back by the shorter road down the hill."

George sat like one in a daze. At length he said:

"I don't think he came back to town. I was about the village during the day and was at the Blue Boar awhile in the forenoon, and did not see him nor hear Jonas say anything about a stranger looking for cattle. He may have gone up the river on this side."

Neither could bear to give expression, even to the other, to their mutual perception of the terrible truth.

The girl arose and walked away some distance and leaned, with averted face, against a tree. When she came back after some minutes, there were traces of tears and she showed profound distress, though striving to be calm.

One thought painful to Holmes, who did not doubt the man had been robbed and murdered, was that he had not been allowed to know anything about the plot. Evidently the landlord of the Blue Boar had played the decoy; and though he had been with Blue repeatedly the past week, on seemingly the friendliest terms of confidence, not a hint of this had been breathed to him. It showed him that he was excluded from the confidence of Harry and his associates; and that meant that since they no longer trusted him they would take measures to secure themselves against the possibility of his betraying what he already knew. Thus dangers were thickening around him, threatening his life or at least a separation from Loraine. He might go away and escape their vengeance; but what would life be worth to him away from her?

Their thoughts were mutually too painful for expression. They sat awhile without speaking and then arose and walked farther down the road to find what relief they could in movement.

"You told me not long ago," she said, at length, "that your Uncle Andy had offered to join you in leasing the Smith farm on Simpson's Creek, and let you work it for what you could make out of it. Have you done anything about it yet?"

"No, Loraine, not yet. The owner wants more rent than we ought to pay. Besides, I don't know where I am to raise money to get the plows and wagons and other farm tools I would need. Father would let me have one of the horses and Uncle Andy another. May be we can see some way to fix it up between now and time for fall seeding."

"You will have to go away," she said; "I see that clearly. It is getting too dangerous for you to stay here."

Her keen vision had pierced the gathering clouds and divined even quicker than his instinct the peril that threatened him.

"I will have to go away or die, Loraine, I know that; but I would rather die than leave you."

She looked at him with humid eyes that spoke unutterable love and her bosom heaved with the emotion inspired by the declaration of his passion; but she said:

"George, that is not a manly way to talk. If you die you leave me, and I lose you forever. You do not need to die; you do not need to leave me except for a time. Go away and try to make a home that I can share with you, where we may begin life anew; no matter where or how poor it may be, if it is your own, though it be only a cabin and a patch; and when you have done this I will come to you and no power on earth shall hold me from you. I can wait and so must you. You know I will be true to you," she added; "only be true to yourself; and be the man that you will be as soon as you get away from here."

She could not say more. Tears came into her beautiful eyes and completed the appeal in language that no man could resist.

"You are right, Loraine, you are an angel!" said her lover, profoundly moved, taking the girl in his arms and kissing her fondly. "I must do it; I will do it. There is no other way; and God helping me, from this hour I will think of nothing but how to bring this about."

She dried her eyes and a happier light came into them; for hope gilds the darkest hour; and for the moment she would fain believe that her lover might be transformed by the greatness of her love, might become worthy of her devotion, might be stimulated by it to work out a future in which she could have a part, away from all these hateful surroundings in which her soul had been cribbed and cabined all her life.

CHAPTER XII.

NEMESIS.

And the Lord said unto Cain, Where is Abel, thy brother? And he said, I know not: Am I my brother's keeper?—Bible.

A month after the declaration of the dividend at the Blue Boar, a paragraph appeared in a Uniontown paper to the effect that Mr. Thomas McKinney, a wealthy citizen of that place, who had gone into Virginia some six weeks before to buy cattle, had not returned nor been heard from, and his family and friends were apprehensive some ill fortune had befallen him. The article described Mr. McKinney, his general appearance and dress and the horse he rode, and stated that he had when he left home a considerable sum of money on his person. A week later the same paper stated that there was not yet any word from the missing man and his family were seriously alarmed for his safety and were making efforts to trace him.

A week later there arrived in the village of Riverside, in the afternoon, by the Fairmont pike, a stranger on horseback, who was dressed and comported himself like a plain citizen on a business trip. He rode up to the Blue Boar and, throwing the rein over a hitching-post, walked into the public room and asked for the landlord. As Blue came out of the bar and confronted the stranger, an unpleasant lump came up in his throat, for he instinctively felt that he knew the man's business before he had told it; but he had himself under good control and did not show the trepidation he really felt. He asked if the stranger would have his horse put up.

"No," was the reply; "at least not yet. I suppose," looking the landlord in the face, "I may speak to you somewhat in confidence."

The latter signified assent.

"I am from Uniontown," said the stranger, "and I am trying to get track of one of my neighbors who came up this way on a business trip about the middle of June. He has not returned within the time his family expected, and at their request I have come to see if I can find him. I have traced him as far as Fairmont, where he stayed at the Mountain City House. The landlord remembers him quite well, and says he told him he was going up in the neighborhood of Clarksburg. I found a man at Worthlesston who thinks he saw him pass through that place; but he was not very clear about it and when I pressed him admitted he was so far away he might be mistaken in the description. Of course, a good many people pass over that road every day, and unless one's attention was specially directed to a passer, his recollection that far back would be vague and uncertain. But I think if he came this far he would likely stop with you and you would recollect him."

The speaker then proceeded to describe the missing man minutely, his personal appearance, dress and the horse he rode. The landlord listened coolly and critically. His confidence had come back. After a pause in which he appeared to be ransacking his memory: "I don't think I ever saw the man. How long ago did you say?"

"About the middle of June as near as I can figure it. The landlord of the Mountain City thought the same."

"I am certain," said Jonas, "there has been no such person here in the last three months, or this year, for that matter, for I could not fail to remember it. We don't have many strangers, and that is a man one would be sure to remember."

The stranger was disappointed. "Is there another hotel here?" he asked.

"Yes, the Busy Bee, just down the street." He stepped to the door and pointed out the building.

"I will leave my horse hitched here and walk down there and make inquiry."

"He won't find out anything there," said the landlord to himself; and he felt a sense of relief that the man was gone.

The landlord of the Busy Bee had not entertained nor heard of the missing traveler. The detective—for such he was—was a man of resources. He reflected and it occurred to him McKinney might have reached the village before night, crossed the river and gone up on the other side. "Is there a ferry here?" he asked.

"Yes."

"What was the state of the river about the middle of June?"

"A man could ride it. There had been a freshet early in the spring, but the river was down again."

"Where can I find the ferryman?"

"I will send a boy to show you," said the obliging landlord of the Busy Bee.

The ferryman was found in his shop on the bank of the river overlooking the ferry. The stranger introduced himself and explained his quest.

"How long ago?" queried the old ferryman.

"Somewhere about the middle of June. It should have been the 15th."

The old man ran over a calculation with the aid of his fingers. "That would be Friday morning. Yes; there was such a man rode down this street to the river just about that time; and I think by looking at a memorandum book I have here I can tell you the exact day, because I was going to Clarksburg that day to buy some hardware at Lowndes', and I had got up early to do some repairing on my boat. I had just got it finished and started up to the house when this man rode down to the edge of the water. He rode in a few steps, and while his horse drank, he turned and asked me if he could ride the river. I told him yes, but he would find it a little deep, and he might get his feet wet. He then asked if I could ferry him. I said I could; so he rode into the boat without getting off his horse, and I went back, pushed off and ran him across. He handed me the pay and rode up the bank. I turned and came right back, and don't remember that I looked around till I had landed and tied the boat. Then as I started to walk up the hill, I turned half round and glanced across at the road above the ferry expecting I would see him somewhere beyond Fontrey's; but I did not see him, and as I had no curiosity in the matter and was thinking of my breakfast and my trip, I came on up home and thought no more of it. This was the man you describe, I am certain. I especially noticed his stylish horse as he stood in the boat; but I could not tell, if it was to save me, whether he went up the river or down."

The old man had all this while been fumbling in a tool-chest, and at last brought out a small account book. He looked it over a few moments. "Yes, I find I went to Clarksburg on the 15th of June. That was Friday, and that was the morning this traveler came down and was ferried over."

"What hour in the morning was this?"

"It was early. I had not had my breakfast yet."

"Where could he have come from?" spoke the stranger, more to himself than to the other.

Then, turning to the ferryman: "He did not stay at either of the hotels in the village. Where would you think he might have stayed over night?"

"Then he must have stayed out of town somewhere and taken an early start."

This appeared to be a solution. "That is it," the stranger said, and thanking the ferryman for his courtesy he walked back to the Blue Boar, unhitched and mounted his horse and rode out of the village by the way he had come.

At this moment Guy Esmond walked down the street and came to the corner door in which the landlord was standing. He saw the man riding away and turned to his friend for an explanation. The latter looked around and, seeing no one near, spoke cautiously: "That man is from Uniontown and is looking for the cattle-buyer who stayed over night some six weeks ago and went over to your place the next morning. You slip right over and let Harry know. May be he had better come up to-night and see me, but not till after dark. You walk down to the mill and cross there."

Less than a mile out of the village on the Fairmont road the stranger stopped at a farm-house on the left which looked as if a man might have asked hospitality there. As he rode into the lane he saw near the barn an old man whom he judged to be the proprietor, giving directions to a colored man, also well along in years. The latter walked to the gate as the stranger rode up, took off an old battered hat, put it under his arm, and made a ceremonious bow. The stranger politely returned the salutation and said he would like to speak with the master. The old man, hearing this, came forward and stood by the gate, while the colored servant stood near by in non-participant attitude but keen of ear for the conversation.

The stranger went over the explanation he had to make and at the conclusion asked if the missing traveler had stayed over night at that house. The old man replied in the negative. Nobody had stayed with them this spring. Had he seen anybody passing that would answer the description? No; possibly Joe had. Then, turning to the colored man:

"Joe, did you see anybody like this ride along, going towards town, about the middle of June? You heard what he was like?"

"Yes, sah," said Joe. "I hear de gemman's 'scription and I think I seed de man. 'Deed I'ze most shuah I did, caze I meet him in de road and have a inte'view with him."

"Tell us about it," said the stranger.

"Yes, sah," said Joe, appreciating his opportunity. "Mars Short he tell me to hitch up de wagon and go to town after de plow which had de pint broke and was at Mistah Stores' shop; and Mistus Mary she tell me be shuah not fo'git to go to post office, fur she were expecting a letter——"

"But tell us about the man," said the stranger, interrupting.

"Yes, sah," said Joe, with a bow; "I tell de gemman in a minute. I got de plow in de wagon and had letter in my hat, and I druv out over the hill and I see a man riding towards me just dis side de fus' holler; and when he come up to me I see he was goin' to say somethin' and I kinder stop de team and he pull up his hoss, and he ast me how fur it were to de town. I tole him soon's he got out on de hill dere he'd see it. Den he ast me if I know of any yearlin' cattle about here for sale."

"Did he," interrupted the stranger, "ride on to the town?"

"He ride in that directium," said Joe, with due caution, as if he were a witness on the stand. "I couldn't say he went all de way; but I 'spect he did, caze when I look around just 'fore I got to de fus' holler he were out of sight." Joe made another bow as if to terminate the "inte'view."

"Do you think that was the man I have described?" the stranger asked.

"I'm shuah it was. He rode a very fine bay critter, and he had a big nose and side whiskers; and he were very polite. And his astin' 'bout de cattle makes me know it were de same gemman you is lookin' foh."

"About what time of day was this?"

"It was gettin' putty late. Come to think, it was quite late in the ebenin', caze I 'member it was dusk when I druv in and unhitched."

The stranger thanked both politely and, mounting, rode away. At the mouth of the lane he was undecided a moment which way to turn, then he rode on east. A quarter of a mile farther he came to a small stream, and here the roads forked. He rode aside under some spreading sycamores and, dismounting and putting his arm through the rein, walked to a foot-bridge that offered a convenient seat and sat down to think over the tangled skein.

Here he had the very positive recollection of two men, neither of whom could possibly have any interest in deceiving him, one showing that McKinney had passed on to the village before nightfall, the other that he had crossed the river at an early hour in the morning—presumptively the next morning. Where did he spend the night? He was within half a mile of the village when the colored man saw him near dusk and left him going in that direction; and there were no houses on the road between that meeting-place and the village. Why had he not stayed at one of the hotels? He was a man accustomed to travel and spend his nights at hotels; and as he knew nobody in the village, it did not seem possible he had asked for private hospitality. Had he gone beyond the village and stayed at some farm-house and returned to the ferry next morning? That was the least probable of all. He must have stayed at one of the hotels. Could the landlords have forgotten? Hardly, for the entertainment of a stranger who would probably make inquiries of them about cattle would be readily recalled where such a guest would be unusual. Could the landlords have any motive for denying his presence? If he had not been seen afterwards this might be suspected. But he did not disappear at a hotel; that was proven by the positive recollection of the ferryman. It was a puzzle.

He sat for a long time revolving these and other thoughts. It was growing dusk and the horse was getting restless at the prospect of spending the night without food. He mounted and rode back to the village and to the Blue Boar.

Mine host was surprised and puzzled at the man's return. He was shown to his room while supper was being prepared for him and the horse sent to the stable. At the moment these dispositions had been made, Harry Esmond walked into the hallway by the side door and he and Jonas met opportunely on the back porch. They went to the den and shut the door.

"What is this, 'Jone,' about a man from Uniontown looking for somebody?"

The landlord lowered his voice. "They are tracing for him and have tracked him as far as Fairmont. They found one man who thinks he saw him ride through Worthlesston, but he is not dead sure. The man came here this afternoon to inquire, but I didn't know the first thing in the world; never saw such a man. Then he went to the Busy Bee, and of course he didn't find out anything there. But he was gone a good while and I've been wondering whether he struck a trail anywhere else. So he came back and mounted and rode away, about a half an hour by sun, in the direction he had come. I thought he had given it up or gone back to Fairmont to get a fresh start; but he has just returned and is up stairs getting ready for supper. I wish I knew what brought him back. When he rode away this afternoon, he never said a word about what he had found out. I wonder if he heard anything from anybody else, and where he went when he rode out the Fairmont pike. When he comes down to supper I will seat him on the far side of the table and you can go around on the back porch and get a good look at him through the windows."

The landlord returned to the public room. The stranger had come down and was immediately preceded to the supper room by the landlord, who drew back a chair and seated the guest facing the windows on the porch. Harry sauntered out on the porch in the dark and, strolling carelessly back and forth past the windows, obtained a good view of the stranger, whose features and demeanor he fixed in his memory as something he might need to be familiar with. The publican bustled about ostensibly to see that his guest was served to his satisfaction, really to give him a chance to ask questions or tell of his discoveries if inclined. But the guest did not seem disposed to talk and gave his whole attention to appeasing his hunger, nor could the landlord bring himself to venture any remark to draw out what he so much wanted to know. At length, rising from the table, the stranger retired at once to his room.

The landlord and Esmond met a few minutes later in the den.

"I don't like his looks," said the latter.

"I'm afraid he has got some clue. I wanted you to see him, because you might want to recognize him in some other place."

"I'd know the fellow in the dark," said Esmond; and in a whisper he added: "He'd better keep on this side of the river. I must go now so as to post the boys to be on the lookout." And then, with rising anger, in a voice incautiously loud: "He had best not fool around here too much, or we won't wait for him to cross the river."

CHAPTER XIII.

AN ABANDONED WELL.

Something is rotten in the State of Denmark.
Cudgel thy brains no more about it.
—Hamlet.

Some ten days after the disappearance of McKinney, two boys from the village who had been ranging the woods on the other side of the river looking for squirrels or other small game, found themselves on top of the great hill back of the old log house occupied by Lot Dyson. Their shortest way towards home lay across the fields on the south slope of the hill; and as they approached the timber belt farther down, which they proposed to enter some distance west of the house, they encountered a thicket covering an acre or two so densely grown with bushes and briers that it looked as if they would have to walk around; but noticing what looked like a path, they entered it, and after a few yards saw on one side a pile of stones that appeared to be the ruins of a chimney.

"Why," said one boy, "I did not know there had ever been a house here."

"It seems to me," observed the other, "I have heard there was an old house in here somewhere that was burned many years ago."

"And what is this?" said the other, drawing back from a pit he had almost fallen into.

It was covered with dead brush, but through this could be seen some half-decayed pieces of timber laid across as if to keep cattle from falling in. Leaning over and peering in through an opening between the timbers, the boys could see that there was an old stone-walled well, with water coming up within ten to fifteen feet of the surface.

"See here," said one, "it looks as if something had gone down."

The brush had been thrust aside and twigs had been broken as if some heavy body had fallen in. Looking more closely, it appeared as if the timbers had been moved and shoved together again.

The boys looked at each other and then at the lonely surroundings with a queer feeling neither could have explained. But the dense thicket cut off the view in all directions, and there was nothing alarming in sight except the dreadful old well, which was only a possible danger to a heedless rabbit hunter plunging through the thicket.

"Let's get away from here. This path doesn't go any farther, and we'd better go back and walk around."

Before the lads got home, the unpleasant feeling they had had about the old well evaporated and they thought little more of it than of other incidents of an unsuccessful morning in the woods.

But at supper one of them asked his father if he remembered an old house in that locality, describing it. The parent replied he had heard there was once a house in there somewheres that had been burned before the Lot Dyson house was built. Some people with a name like Woodfield had lived in it.

"Why did they not build again in the same place?" queried the boy. "It would have saved them digging a well."

"That reminds me of something else," said the father, "that used to be said about it. They would not build again in the same place because the well was spoiled. After those people went away and a new owner came to build he cleared away the rubbish and concluded to clean out the well. They found the body of a man in it who was supposed to have been murdered and thrown in. And that's why, it is said, the next house was built in another place; and there was a story that a ghost used to walk of nights around the old ruins, and that may be why the garden was allowed to go wild and grow up in briers and bushes."

The boy mentioned the finding of that same old well during their morning hunt; and he added that "it looked as if somebody else had been thrown in."

The father smiled at this as a mere boyish terror. There was nothing connected with such a discovery to give it a sinister appearance, and no more was thought of it.

CHAPTER XIV.

ON THE TRAIL.

The patient search and vigil long.
—Byron.

The result of the detective's meditations at the Blue Boar was that he ought to cross the river and see if he could not trace the missing man in that direction. Leaving unsolved the mystery of his night's lodging, it was certain he had gone across the river next morning, and as he was to visit the vicinity of Clarksburg had probably turned up the stream. He would take the road in that direction and make inquiry at farm-houses that he passed. He rose early and told the landlord he would want to set out directly after breakfast; and when he had paid his bill mounted and set off in the direction of the ferry. The landlord was surprised and excited. He was ignorant what information the stranger might have obtained the evening before, and this move excited the wildest conjectures. He felt that a crisis was at hand. Would Harry and his friends be on the lookout this early? He looked around for some means of getting word to Guy, when that convenient person strolled up from the direction of the stable. Beckoning him inside, "Guy," he said, "the stranger has just gone towards the ferry. I don't know what it means—whether he is going to your place or in the other direction. But slip down to the river as quick as you can without attracting attention and see if he crosses and which way he goes."

Guy walked leisurely down the street to the river bluff as if he had the day before him. When he arrived on the bluff, the ferry-boat was just landing on the other side and a passenger on horseback rode up the bank and took the road up the river. Guy looked long enough to be sure of the identity of the traveler and strolled back to the Blue Boar and communicated to Blue what he had seen.

"I don't understand it," Jonas said, "but Harry ought to know."

"I will go right over as soon as I get breakfast," said the accommodating Guy.

A mile above the ferry the traveler came to a prosperous looking farm-house evidently belonging to a large farm. Two or three men were moving about the barn and yard. He rode up to the gate, and one of the younger and better dressed came down to meet him. He explained what he was looking for; and waited, not without anxiety, for the reply. The farmer said he had not heard of any cattle-buyer from a distance. None had been at their place. They did some grazing and were often visited by buyers looking for cattle, but none had been there this spring or summer so far. He could not be sure he was home at the date mentioned, but he called the other men to the gate and asked if anybody had stopped or made inquiry for cattle some six weeks before; and, on their answering in the negative, whether they had seen anybody pass that answered the description which the stranger then repeated to them. None had seen or heard of such a person.

This was discouraging, but it would not do to give it up yet. McKinney might have had some particular place to visit farther up the road and have gone directly thither without stopping on the way. He rode on and two miles farther came to a village with two or three stores and shops. To his inquiries, he received on all hands the same kind of reply. No stranger had been in the village or had passed through, unless in the night. Would he pass this way if he were going to Clarksburg? Yes. Were there any roads on which he might have turned off? Yes, one; he might have turned up Robinson's Run, about two miles back. He went back and turned into this road. A mile or more from the river he came to a hamlet, with a mill, a store and a dozen dwellings. The farms around looked promising and numbers of cattle were grazing on the fresh green grass of the meadows. But the same negative met all his inquiries. The merchant said he could not have failed to know if any stranger had been there or had passed through in the day time, and he had neither seen nor heard of any.

The detective returned to the river road and drew up in the shade for a little reflection. It seemed useless to pursue the quest any farther in this direction. These people could not all be in a conspiracy to give him false answers. There was but one possible conclusion: McKinney had gone the other way—down the river, not up; and while this seemed a rather inexplicable move, no doubt it would be simple enough when understood. Then he must ride down the river and make inquiry, and there he would find the clue.

Unless—the thought darkly crossed his mind—unless there was no clue to be found anywhere. Unless there had been foul play. He had not, with all his experience, set himself seriously to consider this contingency before. But now he faced it resolutely. He had rested in the assumption that some illness or other ordinary misfortune had overtaken McKinney; but, after all, if this had been true, why had not he or some one for him communicated with his family? The absence of all word argued ill. The detective was shaken in the faith he had held up to this moment that McKinney was somewhere in safety, though perhaps not well.

This shadow of evil came over him like a cloud, and out of that cloud came the sinister suggestion that possibly one of the landlords was a party to some net that had entrapped the missing cattle buyer. His thoughts went back to the man of the Blue Boar and he reviewed everything he had said and looked in their interviews. Suspicion sharpens the perceptions. He recalled that at the first meeting he had been conscious of a secret uneasiness in the landlord, felt rather than expressed, and that when he returned and took his horse away, and also when he came back in the evening, the landlord had not asked, as people naturally do under such circumstances, if he had heard anything of his missing neighbor.

He was thinking intensely on this train of suggestion when he came opposite the ferry again, and he stopped under a tree to run out his thoughts to some conclusion before he went farther. He looked at his watch and found it a little past midday. He had almost made up his mind that he had better go on down the river and pursue his inquiries, when he saw the old ferryman come out of his house and proceed to his shop like a man who had just had his dinner. This reminded him of his own hunger, of which he had hardly been conscious, so tense had been his mental stress, and it reminded him also that his horse needed both food and drink. He hailed the ferryman just as he was about to enter his shop and signalled him to bring the boat.

When he had come aboard, the old man asked if he had found any further trace of his missing neighbor. He replied no; but that he had not yet been down the river and it was now evident his neighbor had gone in that direction; that he thought he would go down that way after dinner. The ferryman seemed about to offer some suggestion; but checked himself, as if thinking better of it, and said no more.

CHAPTER XV.

A CHANGE OF BASE.

That's a perilous shot out of an elder gun.
—Henry VI.

The detective rode to the Busy Bee and handed his horse to the ostler. After dinner he went to the stable to see the condition of the animal and to have assurance it had received proper attention. It happened that while he was there, Jacob Holmes, the wagon-maker, came into the yard pulling a buggy he had repaired. He dropped the shafts and after some words with the ostler regarding the work turned to go away, when the stranger, who thought it would do no harm to widen the scope of his inquiries, approached and addressed him. Mr. Holmes was an approachable man, not destitute of curiosity nor averse to any conversation that might gratify it.

"You are pretty well acquainted about this place, I suppose," remarked the stranger.

"Yes; I have lived here several years and know everybody 'round here. But you have the advantage of me."

"My name is Bernard, and I am from Uniontown."

"From Uniontown! I'm glad to see a man from Pennsylvany, for I come from Brownsville myself and knew people at Uniontown, Greensboro, and, in fact, I have sold wagons to people all round in that part of the country. My name is Holmes—Jacob Holmes. My journeyman, Jim English, came from Uniontown. Do you know Robert Dumfries or Balt Kramer?"

"I have heard of Dumfries; I never met him; and I know Kramer, near Greensboro. Did you know Thomas McKinney? He was a farmer, and I think had one farm not far from Brownsville."

"McKinney—McKinney? Yes, I have heard of Thomas McKinney. He had cattle farms and grazed a good deal?"

"Yes. Well, McKinney came up this way about six weeks ago and was expected back in three weeks. He has not been heard of. He came to buy cattle, and had considerable money with him. I am one of the neighbors, and came up to see if I could get any information about him."

"Is that so?" said Holmes, with interest. Have you heard anything?"

"He left Fairmont, they told me at the Mountain City House, and came this way, they think on the 14th of June, for the register shows he stopped there the evening of the 13th; and he crossed the river here early next morning."

"If he made any speed and came straight on," remarked Holmes, "he should have got here by the middle of the afternoon."

"I have reason to believe that he reached here late in the evening. I cannot learn where he stayed over night. It appears he did not stop at either of your hotels; but as he crossed on the ferry here at early breakfast time the next morning, he must have stayed in this village or near by."

"Did he cross the river?"

"Yes, the ferryman remembers it well; and he must have gone down the river on the other side, for I have been up the country on that side and could not hear of him."

This suggested something to Holmes, who hesitated and looked around. The ostler had gone back to the house. The old wagon-maker drew nearer to Bernard and, sinking his voice, said: "I can tell you something. I went to the mill early on Friday morning just about the time you speak of—and I think it was that Friday; I could tell at my shop, for my book will show a credit to the miller for feed I got of him that morning—and as I came back I saw a man on horseback ride off the ferry-boat and take the road down the river."

The detective was electrified. "Could you describe his appearance?"

I was not near enough to tell much about the man. He was a plainly dressed, farmer looking man. The most I noticed was that his horse, a bright bay, carried himself up very stylishly, and was a pacer."

"That must have been McKinney. Where should you think he would be going?"

"You say he has not been heard of since?"

"No."

"I am afraid he did not go very far. I don't know what to think." Holmes seemed a good deal agitated. "There's some bad people around here, and it is not very safe for us who live here to say much about them."

Bernard was intensely interested. He waited for the old man's further speech. Holmes drew nearer and said in an agitated whisper: "I don't dare tell you what I fear. If you go down the river to look for McKinney, keep a sharp lookout. It will be better for you not to go—at least not by yourself. And don't tell a soul that you had any talk with me about it."

The speaker turned abruptly and walked away, leaving Bernard astonished at what the old man had told him and no less at his manner of telling it.

Bernard went back to the house and asked for a room, went to it, sat down and took his head between his hands and sat there motionless for a long time. With these new revelations, he tried to go over the whole ground again; to look at the facts, piece by piece, and put them together again; and he saw that a mystery of the profoundest interest and of dark colors was opening before him. What and where was the danger that Holmes had warned him against? Plainly, whatever and wherever it was, it was connected with the disappearance of McKinney.

And now he was confirmed in his opinion that McKinney had stayed at one or other of the village hotels. He reviewed the incidents and conversations of the two days; and when he had finished the review he saw that the first thing for him to do was to satisfy himself which of the publicans had taken the stranger in. He went down stairs and sauntered into the bar and engaged the landlord in conversation. The man talked freely and naturally, without any restraint, asking what he had learned, if anything, to account for his missing neighbor, and trying with a native curiosity to find out something about himself. Clearly there was no occasion for suspicion in this quarter. The more he reflected, the more he was convinced the man at the Blue Boar knew more of McKinney than he was willing to tell; that the cattle-buyer had stayed there over night and had probably acted on some suggestion when he went next morning at such an early hour down the river and into oblivion.

In the evening, after an early tea, he walked up the street to the Blue Boar corner. Several loungers were on the pavement and on a bench at the end of the house. The landlord himself was standing in the corner door leaning against the jamb, and was manifestly ill at ease under the keen scrutiny with which Bernard favored him. He merely said "good evening" and Bernard returned the salutation. The conversation of the loungers was suspended; and to relieve the awkwardness of the situation Bernard approached the person nearest and politely asked to be directed to the postoffice. The building just across the street was pointed out to him and he walked over and asked if there was a letter for Mark Bernard. There was none (as he knew) and he returned down the street. Taking the other side he joined a group in front of a store just across from the Busy Bee. It was the usual evening assembly to discuss affairs, local and national. As he came up he heard allusion to the inquiries made for a missing man and to the ferryman's report that he had crossed the river. He passed into the store and got a cigar and came back and stood in the door while he lighted it. There was evident restraint in the talk, due either to his presence or to other reason, but one man spoke out boldly:

"If he had any money with him he'd better have stayed on this side of the river."

Clearly the other side of the river was dangerous territory. Bernard noted the speaker and crossed to the hotel. A half hour later he met this man in the growing dusk on the hotel pavement, and catching his eye advanced and introduced himself as a person in search of the missing man who had been alluded to in the conversation across the street. "Would you mind telling me, in confidence," he said, "why you said what you did about the danger of carrying money on the other side of the river?" The other, who seemed a rather keen, intelligent man, drew Bernard to one side.

"If you can keep the counsel I give you," he said, "I don't mind telling you to be on your guard in any inquiries you push here in the village or hereabouts regarding the missing cattle-buyer. There is a gang in this neighborhood that is not above killing a man for money, and it is possible your friend has fallen into their clutches. Their headquarters are the farm next below on the other side of the river. If you are sure he went that way, I should be afraid he never got past that farm. Have you reason to think he went to their place for anything?"

Bernard replied that was what he feared. Seeing he could talk freely to this man, he proceeded to tell him about his inquiry at the hotels to learn if McKinney had stayed at either on a certain Thursday night in June before the ferryman set him over the river next morning, and the negative statement of both landlords.

"This landlord here," said the other, "is all right. Whatever he told you was the truth."

"How about the other?" asked Bernard.

"I don't say anything about him; but if your friend crossed the river Friday morning as early as the ferryman says, depend upon it he stayed in this town over night; and I don't believe he would go to a private house when there were two hotels open. If he did, we would have heard of it before this, for the town has been talking about the matter all day."

"Would you advise me to go down the river to the place you speak of and make inquiry?"

"By no means, unless you had a sheriff's posse behind you. Being on your guard, you might do it and come away safely; but you would get no information and there would be nothing to pay you for the risk. We here are all afraid to say much about this gang. While we know a good deal, and believe a great deal more, in regard to their deviltry, it is hard to get evidence that we could act on. It is risky even to talk openly about them, for they have connections and spies in the town and we never know when our words may be repeated at headquarters."

"Could you give me the name by which this gang is known and particularly the one who is the head or leader?"

"Esmond is the name of the family who own the farm, and Harry Esmond is the leader."

"I am very greatly indebted to you," said Bernard, seeing the other was inclined to close the conversation.

"Let me tell you one thing more," said the other, recalling him. "If our surmises are correct as to the fate that has overtaken your friend, it being known you are here tracing for him, you will be in constant danger, in the village or out of it."

"Thank you for the caution," returned Bernard as they parted.

He went to his room overwhelmed at the ramifications and turpitude of the plot that was unfolding. He lay down on the bed without undressing, without making a light, not to sleep but to consider these latest aspects of the problem that confronted him. He did not for a moment question the truth of what had just been told him. It more than corroborated what had been said by Holmes. The hint regarding the landlord of the Blue Boar confirmed his own suspicion. Manifestly the publican had played the part of decoy; had given McKinney false information or some concocted story that had lured him into a trap prepared for him.

But was not Bernard traveling too fast towards conclusions? How should the landlord do this when McKinney only got there at dark and left early next morning? What could the landlord know about him or how confer with confederates across the river in so short a time? Then it occurred to him that McKinney's family had said he had been advised to come to this village; and it seemed to him that they said a particular hotel had been mentioned at which it would be best for him to stop. This had to be considered. Could there be a conspiracy reaching as far as that? Accustomed as Bernard had been to unravel the tangled webs of criminal life, he was a little startled by this idea, that here was a band with agents in another state making suggestions of false information to lure men who carried money in the course of their honest business into snares laid for them, with spies and agents at every point where needed to direct the steps of the unwary to their death!

Bernard lay till midnight without even changing his position, so tense and absorbing was the turmoil of his thoughts. Then he rose and undressed; and, recalling the caution he had received, turned the key in the lock and laid his revolver under his pillow. But before dropping into the uneasy slumber that filled the rest of the night, he plainly saw the futility of any further prosecution of his quest in the manner he had begun it. It would take time, he would need help, and the problem must be approached in another way. He would return to Uniontown and with the help of information to be supplied by the family see if he could pick up a thread at that end of the line.

Next morning, having reached definite conclusions and a settled purpose, he set out on his return, passing up to the Fairmont road at the street intersection in front of the Blue Boar. The landlord was out sweeping the pavement and saw him turn the corner to the north. A moment later he went to the stable whither Guy had just gone with the ostler. "Put the saddle and bridle on Sam," he said in a peremptory way that meant he wanted it done quick. He drew Guy to one side. "Mr. Detective has started back to Fairmont. Guess he's had enough of this town. Take Sam and ride over and let Harry know. He may want to say farewell to the fellow so he will know he need not come again. Johnson could take the short cut and meet him in the woods at Riley Hill. He ought to take a little lead with him back to Uniontown as a keepsake."

An hour later as Bernard was riding leisurely up the hill leaving the river a mile or so south of Worthlesston, busy with his thoughts and scarcely noticing his surroundings, he was startled by the crack of a rifle in the bushes near by and the simultaneous whistle of the ball. He felt his coat twitch and looking down saw that the bullet had passed through both coat and vest within two inches of his heart. He first thought that some careless squirrel hunter had come perilously near killing the wrong game. A moment later he thought of the Esmond gang and of the warning that had been given him. He put whip to the horse and rode rapidly over the hill.

When he stopped to pay toll at the Worthlesston bridge, he asked the gatekeeper, showing him the bullet-holes, if travelers on the roads hereabouts were required to pay for the privilege of being shot at? The old gateman, totally incapable of understanding a jest, replied that all he paid for was going over the road and that the shooting was no part of the road regulations; and he turned and pointed to the printed rules posted up beside the gate. Bernard smiled at the old man's simplicity and rode on.

CHAPTER XVI.

TURNING A NEW LEAF.

Oh, reform it altogether.
—Hamlet.

George Holmes had reached the crisis of his life. He felt it as he had never felt anything before. The pleading, impassioned words of Loraine—her pale face, her tears; above all, her appeal to his manhood, and her promise to follow him to the ends of the earth whenever he had shown himself worthy of her respect and love—had stirred the fountains of feelings that had for years been sealed in the lad's soul. It was as if scales had dropped from his eyes, and he saw with the clear sight of truth and conscience the monstrous life he had been leading, and also the despicable weakness and pusillanimity that had overgrown his real and better self. Days passed in the struggle over the revelation and the disturbance wrought by it in the whole tenor of his being.

He took early occasion to converse with his father and under pledge of absolute secrecy told him the whole story of his connection with the Esmonds, his participation in some of their lawless deeds and his knowledge of others in which he had no part. A new leaven was working in the boy's heart, and day by day he grew more determined and more impatient to find a place to begin the new life he was pledged to and resolved on. In his new character as a man of purpose and action, he determined that he would not see Loraine again. He would not risk his new strength by putting himself under the spell that seemed always to disarm him of every desire in the world except the wish never to leave her. He would when he was ready to go away write her a parting word.

He left home one morning and walked to the farm of his uncle Andy Morrow, a half dozen miles distant. "Uncle Andy," he said to his kinsman at the first opportunity, "I have come up to see if you cannot give me some work on the farm and if you will not let me stay here and work till the holidays. I will work faithfully and earn my wages if you will pay me the same as the other hands."

"Uncle Andy," who had a soft place in his heart for the lad and had grieved over his obliquities, was glad to hear him say this. "George, do you really mean it?"

"As God is my judge," he replied. "I have turned over a new leaf and I only want a chance to begin. Try me."

"You shall go to work Monday morning, and I will pay you the same as the others."

"All I ask," said George, "is that you will pay me up at New Year's, for then I will want to go home and will have need of the money."

"That will be all right; but you will want to go home oftener than that?"

"No; and I would like just as few people as possible to know that I am here," speaking in a subdued manner.

"All right."

CHAPTER XVII.

DIGGING APPROACHES.

Smooth runs the water where the brook is deep.
—Henry VI.

A fortnight to three weeks after the return of Mr. Mark Bernard to Uniontown, there arrived at Walker's hotel in Clarksburg a good looking, keen-eyed man who might be thirty years old, with trunk and stylish leather hand-bag, who registered the name of "Allan St. George, Baltimore." For a day or two he moved quietly about the hotel, or sat in the reading room, reading or writing letters. He had the poise, the quiet demeanor, the courtesy toward strangers, that mark the man who has knocked about the world and worn off the rough corners. He dressed in good taste without display save a single diamond of rare luster, evidently of great value, worn in his tie.

The weather being fine, he walked around the town a little, visiting the other hotels and loitering in their offices and reading rooms, as a man will who has a little more leisure on his hands than he knows what to do with. Then he procured a horse and buggy from the livery and drove out on the country roads—up the Weston pike, out towards Buckhannon, down the Fairmont pike towards Riverside. One Sunday he climbed to the summit of Pinnickinick and spent an hour or so in the enjoyment of the lovely landscape that spread beneath that lofty outlook.

One of the first acquaintances he made was "Uncle Jim" Bartlett, the host of the Bartlett Hotel—probably as unique and interesting a character as Clarksburg ever produced. He found the old man a mine of information about nearly everything he wanted to know and often dropped into his office to chat with him. There were numerous ties, business and social, between Clarksburg and Baltimore, and Uncle Jim was always glad to see a

Baltimore man, even if he did not happen to know personally any of his Baltimore acquaintances.

St. George did not push himself on anybody; but, as he was a pleasant looking and pleasant spoken gentleman, he began to pick up friendly acquaintances about the hotels and elsewhere. There will always be found a few persons curious to know something about the personal affairs of a stranger. Mr. St. George met some of these; and he knew just how to answer their inquiries, with both reserve and candor, to make them feel he had confided to them the actual state of his business and intentions. It soon became understood around the town that he was a man of means and not averse to making some investments in or about the old Harrison County town—perhaps in grazing lands or coal lands; possibly in the establishment of a bank if he found there was room for another. There was just enough vagueness in the plans thus disclosed to make him an object of interest. A young man who has money to place will not lack for opportunities or advice. He will be sought by people who have property to sell, or marriageable daughters to get rid of, or speculative schemes to promote promising enormous returns but requiring just a little more capital; or, last, by the devotees of sport, who know sure ways to add to his wealth by the opportunities to be found at such places as the gaming-table or the race-track. St. George soon found himself courted by these various interests. He was invited out in a social way, and was the cynosure of many bright eyes at the Pike street church he attended on Sabbath. He saw he was getting too popular in the upper circles and withdrew somewhat from the glare of so much favor. His purposes did not lie in that direction.

All the while he had been, as much as he dared, pushing his acquaintance with the sports of the town. He was on all proper occasions free with money and ready to pay for cigars and drinks for those who would indulge—and there is no shorter cut than this to the good will of the average "sport." He gave them to understand they were more to his taste than the "upper crust" who were inclined to take him up. While he seemed more than willing to get acquainted with everybody in sporting circles, he was timid about the risks they offered him and posed somewhat in the role of a "tenderfoot;" which made him all the more interesting to these acquaintances. It was not long before he was able to divide them into two groups: the non-professional, who were getting rid of their money; and the professional, who were acquiring it. He was surprised to find so many expert gamblers in this small town; but he soon discovered it was a sort of center for the towns and country behind it, and drew largely on the resources of this tributary region, embracing places like Weston, Glenville, Sutton, Buckhannon, Beverly and Phillippa. For he began to be introduced to gentlemen from these places, who found the attractions of Clarksburg not confined to the landscape and other surface pulchritudes. There were lawyers and judges, and doctors and capitalists, and others who were none of these, that were not averse to a game and who did not scorn to profit by their skill at the expense of the less expert visitors from the "back counties" who stopped over night as they passed between their mountain homes and the commercial cities beyond.

These professionals and experts thought they were drawing St. George into their nets. He, complete master of himself and of his plans, when only using them to forward purposes of his own, the first of which was to get familiar with all the shady people he could find in that vicinity.

There is a sort of freemasonry in vice and crime, with unperceived grips and invisible signs, connecting their votaries by strong but intangible ties. One looking for a horse-thief or murderer, will not go far astray if he seeks him in the haunts of the gambling fraternity. He would have taken another long step toward his goal when he got to know intimately the frequenters of the race-course. People who steal, or who murder for money, nine times in ten find their compensation at the gaming-table or the race-track.

St. George was quietly but rapidly making himself familiar with the seamy side of the old county town. In these circles he assumed more and more the air of a sport and manifested a little more reckless and adventurous disposition than he would have cared to show in other circles. From time to time he accepted the invitations of gentlemen from other towns, and visiting them, renewed these acquaintances and made others; all the while delving deeper and deeper into that predatory substratum of society which subsists by excursions beyond the moral and statutory codes. In a surprisingly short time, considering the magnitude and difficulty of the task, and without apparent special effort (though really as the result of prodigious study and activity), he knew nearly all the equivocal characters in two or three counties.

One night he was introduced to a Mr. Keifer, who he learned divided his time and talents between Clarksburg and Buckhannon and some other less conspicuous localities. They became good friends with great speed. St. George had heard of Keifer as an intimate ofHarry Esmond, and the acquaintance would be a step towards his aim. Keifer thought St. George might be a goose that he could pluck. As the friendship grew, St. George regaled Keifer with stories of his adventures in the East, some of them very wild (for St. George was gifted with a ready invention), and Keifer, in return, told of some bold strokes whereby he had gotten on the blind side of dame fortune. He mentioned his acquaintance with Esmond and wanted St. George to meet him as soon as it could be brought about. St. George expressed the great pleasure it would give him to meet Mr. Esmond, without showing a shade of the solicitude he felt to bring about this very result. He gave Keifer to understand that he had at command considerable money, if he could find a way to employ it profitably, and asked him to keep an eye out for ventures that might offer beyond what he would desire for himself. Such friendships ripen quickly when both parties concur in applying the necessary warmth. At the end of a week Keifer would have sworn he had known St. George a year, and that he knew him inside and out, from top to bottom, as a prince of good fellows.

The morning after the first meeting with Keifer, St. George wrote in his room a report to his chief, Mr. Mark Bernard, Pittsburg, in which occurred this passage:

"I have at last made the acquaintance of a man who is an intimate of Esmond's and I think a member of the gang. Through him I feel sure I shall soon secure a meeting with Esmond under favorable auspices."

One night Keifer had a friend with him, whom he introduced to St. George as Mr. Tarbert—"a friend, by the way," he added, "of Harry Esmond." This acquaintance was another step forward and the pleasure it gave St. George lent such a charm to his manner towards Tarbert that the latter was delighted and told Keifer afterwards that St. George was the "nicest fellow" he had ever met. Tarbert told them there was to be a day's races at Sardis, a small village on Tenmile, a few miles west of Clarksburg, in which neighborhood it appeared Mr. Tarbert had his home. He invited them to come over and see the sport.

"I wonder if Harry will be there?" asked Keifer.

"I think he will," replied Tarbert. "If you would like to see him I will send him word and perhaps he will come."

"I would like to see him," Keifer said. "I have some things I want to talk over with him, and I would like him to meet Mr. St. George."

St. George expressed the great pleasure this would give him. He was not sure but some matters of business might recall him to Baltimore about that time; but if he could arrange it, he would go to Sardis and see the races.

The day for the races arrived. St. George found the Baltimore business could wait. He hired the best livery team he could get in the town and, with Keifer, drove across the country to Sardis. They went to the

Ogden House and had the horse fed and got dinner. They soon met Tarbert, who introduced them to numerous friends. One was Lynn Johnson, who, in answer to Tarbert's inquiry, said Esmond would be there but it might be the middle of the afternoon before he would arrive. A little after two o'clock Keifer caught sight of Esmond riding into the village. He rode up to the hotel in front of which they were standing and descending gave Keifer a cordial greeting. Keifer turning to St. George, said:

"Harry, I want you to know a friend of mine, Mr. St. George, of Baltimore, who is a man after your own heart."

Esmond turned with beaming cordiality: "Mr. St. George, I am glad to know any friend of Keifer's. He is such a bear that when he endorses a man I know he must have unusual merit."

St. George was flattered by his reception, and on his part showed just enough delicate deference to complete the conquest begun by Keifer's flattering introduction.

After a little chat Esmond moved about to find Tarbert and other friends, and at three o'clock they went to the race track. It was a half-mile course and there were five entries: Nancy Jane, Blue Bell, Fanny Ellsler, Spotted Horse and Dandy Jim.

"Old Spot," said Johnson, "used to be a bird. I have ridden him myself and have won good money; but he is getting a little stiff."

St. George put a $20 gold piece on Nancy Jane; and to his surprise, he won. Esmond did not bet on the first race; but on the next he bet $50 on Blue Bell, and was also a winner. Johnson lost $10 on Dandy Jim.

St. George, keeping up his role of tenderfoot, did not bet again; but Esmond won $100 on the last race by laying it on Fanny. Pleased with his good luck, he led the way to the hotel and ordered drinks. When St. George poured out about a spoonful in his glass, Tarbert noticed it and looked around and smiled.

"Al. is a sort of tenderfoot," said Keifer; "you mustn't mind it." (St. George had told Keifer he was called "Al." among his familiars.)

"Don't despise me, gentlemen," said St. George. "I've been trying all my life to learn to drink, and I can't do it. I haven't the head for it."

"Don't feel bad about it," laughed Esmond; "I'm in the same boat. Some of my boys will drink as much in one minute as I can in a month."

St. George looked at his youthful face with a touch of surprise. "Your 'boys'? Have you any boys old enough to drink?"

"O," said Harry, flushing a little, "I haven't any boys of my own—at least none that I acknowledge," smiling. "I meant some of my friends. Johnson here is one of them. Look at his glass (which he had filled to the brim). Now Johnson isn't a very big man, but that kind of a drink never staggers him."

Johnson was a little dashed, but he came well out of it.

"You see," he said, turning to St. George, "I drink so much at Harry's expense that I have got into this 'full habit' through trying to see that he gets the worth of his money. I sacrifice myself to my conscience, for it makes me unpopular with the barkeepers."

"I'll keep you company this time," said Harry, pouring a spoonful into his glass; and he proposing the health of their new friend, Mr. St. George, they all emptied their glasses.

"Abe," said Esmond, "it is getting towards evening, and I have a long ride. Why can't you and Mr. St. George go home with me and stay over Sunday?"

"The fact is," said Keifer, "I have some matters I want to talk over with you, and if it would be agreeable to Mr. St. George to go, I should be glad to do it."

St. George assured both nothing could give him more pleasure; but what would the livery keeper think if his team did not come back this evening?

"Yonder is a Clarksburg man," said Keifer. "I'll send word by him that we have gone down the river and will be back Sunday evening."

"That is it," said Harry. "That will suit all round. So it is settled and let's be off." Turning to St. George, he added:

"You'll have to take pot-luck. You will find plain people and rough fare at our house, but you will be as welcome as if we could offer you a royal palace."

"Never fear," said St. George; "the welcome is all I care for."

CHAPTER XVIII.

BEARING THE CROSS.

Canst thou . . . . .
Pluck from the memory a rooted sorrow;
And with some sweet, oblivious antidote
Cleanse the stuffed bosom of that perilous stuff.
Which weighs upon the heart?
—Macbeth.

After her parting with George Holmes —after she had spoken her heart to him so unreservedly (and, had she known it, so effectively), Loraine Esmond felt some sense of shame lest she had overstepped the delicate boundary of maiden modesty. Yet she had felt then, and still believed, that a crisis had been reached in their lives which made plain speaking and a clear understanding of their relations to each other imperative. At times she had a feeling that she had touched his pride and aroused in him something that he had long been a stranger to.

Days passed, and weeks, yet she saw no more of him nor had any word from him. She realized that his safety forbade his coming to their house, but she thought he might have sent her some word. She knew nothing of the struggle he was going through nor of his heroic resolution; but she believed she had set a leaven at work that would stir his manhood if she had not been mistaken in believing he was still susceptible to the redeeming influence of shame. Thinking of him thus, she felt hopeful and could wait.

When she contemplated at home the awful crime she believed—almost knew—had been committed by those nearest her in ties of consanguinity, she experienced a horror and infinite humiliation that no philosophy she could appeal to would relieve. To make her distress the harder to bear, she had to bear it alone and in secret; there was none with whom she could share her thoughts—to whom she might have confided her agonies and tears.

One day she heard one of her brothers and Harris speaking of some one who had "gone away." These two words were all she had clearly caught. She conjectured it was George, and wondered he had not at least sent her a word of farewell. A day or two later she heard Harris tell her brother that George was "working at Uncle Andy's;" and he added something she did not hear. There was comfort in this; for while she knew nothing of his plans, it showed he was in the right path. She was a little afraid, however, that those who had reason to fear him might not leave him undisturbed.

Loraine Esmond, though favored with few opportunities of education, had acquired more than most girls do under like disadvantages. The most symmetrical body may be dwarfed or deformed by unfavorable conditions, but the mind that is nobly born reaches out through penury or misfortune and puts aside obstacles of every nature to grasp the sustenance required to nourish it for its divine mission; and it finds light, inspiration and knowledge where grosser spirits only grope in darkness and sink under the wretchedness of their condition.

This family had not always been given over to the world, the flesh and the devil. There were some books about the old house, some of them of the few great books which have embodied the most beautiful thoughts and the noblest truths that have enriched human literature. These she had assimilated as her natural food and they had filled her soul with beauty and her mind with thoughts that lifted her far above the degradation of her home. With the same intuitive reaching out for light she absorbed the intelligence brought by the newspapers and was well informed of the world's current events. So that, indeed, in her circle there were few with better and happier opportunities who were her equal in mental elevation, unconscious of it as she was herself.

Of late, in utter weariness of soul, she had often wished for the wings of a dove that she might fly away and be at rest. Daily tasks are hard and existence is cheerless when there is lacking the daily inspiration of joy or content; and yet it is these angels of necessity that in such times of stress deliver our sanity from wreck. She often felt as if the wearisome, monotonous, ever repeated tasks of the house were more than she could bear; yet she did bear them, and hard as they were, they diverted her thoughts into healthier channels and relieved the strain that must otherwise have slain her.

One Saturday night Harry came home in the middle of the night bringing two men with him. She heard them talking and thought one of the voices was familiar; the other she could not recognize. Next morning when Harry came to the kitchen, she asked him who the vistors were. He replied "Abe and a Mr. St. George." At the instant a frightful thought flashed into her mind and made her feel faint: Was this another victim lured to the slaughter for his money? But she asked: "Who is Mr. St. George?"

"He is a gentleman from Baltimore, a friend of Abe's who came over to the races with him. As I wanted to talk with Abe, and St. George seemed such a nice fellow, I invited him to come down and stay over Sunday. You will like him."

"Perhaps," she said, indifferently; but her first fear was dissipated.

At breakfast Harry introduced Mr. St. George to his mother and sister. Keifer needed no introduction. Loraine, without appearing to, observed Mr. St. George very keenly, and her impressions confirmed her brother's words. St. George on his part seemed attracted by the girl, and as much as was perfectly well-bred allowed her to see his respectful admiration. She noticed Keifer addressed him sometimes familiarly as "Al." and saw that he was not a lamb brought to the slaughter but probably one who was to be drawn into participation in their life of lawlessness and crime. This thought was scarcely less terrible to her than the other; for when she looked into his handsome, pleasant face, his clear eye and open brow, and felt the influence of his gracious manners, she felt what a pity it would be that such a man should be brought down to such a life.

During the morning, St. George accompanied Harry and Keifer in their walks about the place and Loraine saw him again only at the midday dinner. He was unmistakably interested in her and would have been glad of an opportunity to converse with her. He thought he saw shame and distress written in the pale face and downcast eyes, and knowing what he did of her surroundings thought he understood the cause of it, and was moved by a profound pity for one who with such a lovely personality was worse than an alien in her own home. Loraine perceived something of St. George's sense of her position and under happier conditions she would have liked to talk to him. But she avoided any conversation. Her heart was too full; she could not trust herself to speak with a stranger whose sympathy was so plainly expressed in eye and manner. She only prayed that for his own sake she might never see him again in that place.

After dinner, St. George excusing himself to Harry and Keifer, who he knew wanted an opportunity for some talk of their own, walked down to the river and strolling along its bank smoked his cigar and admired the magnificent proportions of the great elm. His own thoughts were painful; for he saw that this home of lawlessness hid a direr tragedy than the one he had come to track; and for an instant he got a wider view than he had ever had before of the awful desolation wrought by crime, devouring the lives not alone of its immediate victims but of other innocent victims near and far.

About the middle of the afternoon, St. George's team was brought out and he and Keifer entered, and making their adieus, drove down the lane. Loraine was standing at an open window. St. George seeing her, bowed and lifted his hat, and bowing in return she withdrew to spend the rest of the day in her room.

CHAPTER XIX.

A SOCIAL CALL.

The fattest hog in Epicurus' sty.

—Mason.

When shall we three meet again?

—Macbeth.

In passing down to the Esmond place Saturday night, Esmond and his friends had gone down the west side of the river. On the return of St. George and Keifer Sunday afternoon, they drove through the river and passed up through the pretty village of Riverside, lying on a gentle slope running back from river to hill. This was the nearest route and here they would strike the Fairmont pike, a stoned and graded road running their way. Besides, Keifer wanted to speak a moment to the landlord of the Blue Boar; and this fitted in with St. George's wishes, for Bernard had told him about this gentleman and he felt some solicitude to have a look at him.

They drove up to the pavement and Blue came out.

"Why, hello, Abe, is that you?" was his greeting.

"What is left of me," responded Keifer. "'Jone,' I want you to know a friend of mine, Mr. St. George, of Baltimore. Al., this is Mr. Blue, the owner of that big hog you see up there," pointing to the sign and laughing.

St. George looked up at the picture of the beast. "Where did you get the color?" and he looked smilingly at Blue.

"O," said Jonas, "he used to be black, but hard times made him blue—same as the landlord." It was Blue's turn to laugh now at his witticism and the others joined him in his merriment.

"Will you 'light, gentlemen?" asked the publican.

"No," returned Keifer, "we must be getting on; we have a livery team that we promised to get home this evening. We have been down spending the Sunday with Harry."

Blue looked at St. George with interest.

"Came down with him last night from Sardis races. Anything new?"

"No; same old story except people are getting worked up a little over the election."

"How is it going?" asked Keifer.

"O, we're all for Breckinridge and Lane down here, except a few Black Republicans who swear they are going to vote for Abe Lincoln. They'd better try it. Did you have any luck at Sardis?"

"Didn't bet. You know I never do—when I haven't the money. Harry won $150 and my friend here raked in a twenty. Blue took another look at St. George. "That's just Harry's luck," he said.

"And Lynn lost $10," added Keifer.

"Just his luck, too," said Blue. "All he had, I'd bet."

"Anything I can do for you in Clarksburg?" asked Keifer, gathering up the reins.

"No, don't know of anything. I may be up there some day this week."

"Come and see me," said Keifer. "I'm staying at the Dent."

"I will."

They drove away, Keifer nodding goodbye, St. George politely lifting his hat.

This was a man St. George was glad to get a look at and he had scrutinized him keenly without seeming to do so.

On the dozen miles drive that followed Keifer talked volubly and with apparent unreserve; yet St. George could perceive a certain wariness he had not observed in him at any time before. St. George took pains to respond fully to Keifer's effusiveness and to appear unconscious that any veil, even the gauziest, had been drawn between them. In his report to Bernard, written that night, he said:

"I went with Esmond's friend Keifer to the races at Sardis, Saturday. Esmond was there and on a very cordial invitation went home with him and spent the greater part of to-day looking around their place. I am not able to report much progress. Esmond is no ordinary man. He knows how to hold people off as well as how to attract them. I have no idea he suspected my business, but I think he put Keifer on his guard. Esmond probably acquainted him with reasons he did not know of before for being extra careful. Esmond has a sister who seems a very superior girl, clearly out of sympathy with the rest of the family, and unless I greatly mistake she is in keen distress over some recent occurrence, the nature of which you can guess. She avoided me and would not give me a chance to talk with her. This was the only sign I could discover of anything out of the ordinary. On the return we stopped a few minutes at the Blue Boar and I had a good look at the landlord. There is something sinister about the man and your suspicion is justified."

CHAPTER XX.

ON GUARD.

Beware the Ides of March.
—Julius Caesar.

The Chief of the Esmond band felt that the disappearance of a man of as much consequence as McKinney, carrying as much money as he did and having extensive connections at home, could not but be followed by a determined effort to unearth those who had made way with him. It was no time to be careless or take the risk of fresh exploits. Before engaging in new enterprises, it was prudent to be sure this inquiry had blown over. He accordingly warned his followers to "lay low," as Uncle Remus would put it, to be discreet and on their guard.

A danger that disturbed Esmond which must be carefully watched was the disclosures that appeared to have been made by young Holmes to his father. The exact extent of these could not be known. It did not yet appear whether George had told more or had but given hints that had been repeated. It was clear that he must not be taken into further confidence till it could be ascertained how far he had turned traitor, whether he could be ultimately restored to confidence or whether they must protect themselves against further revelations by sterner measures. If Holmes was disposed to betray them, this quest for McKinney—if pushed energetically and openly; especially if a reward were offered or immunity promised any one disclosing the secrets of the gang—would afford the opportunity for him to make his renunciation of them effective. It was necessary to keep him under surveillance for a time the better to judge whether he had any such purpose. The fact that he had left the village and gone to work indicated some new purpose on his part, but as the watch set over his movements reported that he stayed right on his uncle's farm and apparently saw no strangers, and as there were no further reports of his outgivings, this feeling was somewhat relieved. Holmes was keeping quiet like the others.

It was in line with this policy that Esmond had given a hint to Keifer that there were present reasons for extra caution; that a detective had been in the neighborhood not long before on the track of a man who was supposed to have disappeared in that vicinity (Keifer guessed what this might mean), and it was well to be more than ordinary careful till the matter had "blowed over."

CHAPTER XXI.

A FLANK MOVEMENT.

To leave this keen encounter of our wits.
—Richard III.

Less than a week after his report, St. George received a note from Bernard suggesting that he come to Pittsburgh for a consultation. Bernard, the reader will have divined, was not the real name of the gentleman who had asked for a letter at the Riverside postoffice, nor was St. George the real name of his correspondent; for one was the head of the Duquesne Detective Bureau, and the other his auxiliary; but these names will do for the purpose of this history.

Packing his traveling bag, St. George went down to the office and told Mr. Walker he was going away for a short time. At this moment, Mrs. Walker, sprightly, buxom and youthful for her years, came into the office and saw him standing bag in hand.

"Why, Mr. St. George, not going to leave us?"

"For a few days, much to my regret."

"Well, don't stay long; because if you do," and she looked at him archly, "there will be some disconsolate maidens 'all forlorn' in this old town."

"You are a gay deceiver, Mrs. Walker, to play on my vanity in this way. You are like one of the three graces."

"Which one?"

"Hope."

"Let me see," she said, musingly, "if I remember Hope is represented as a young, good-looking woman."

"Yes, but that is not the only resemblance," smiling at her wit.

"What is another?"

"Why, you know, she 'told a flattering tale.' "

"Yes, and nobody abused her for doing it, as you do me. Now I would like to ask you one—"

"Pardon me; I'm afraid I shall miss my train." The omnibus was at the door.

"O, the train can wait," she said.

"I am sorry you're going to-day, Mr. St. George. The Riverside band is to be here this evening and is going to serenade 'Extra Billy,' who is staying at Judge Camden's. If you will stay I'll have them come around and serenade you. St. George sounds as well as 'Extra Billy,' I am sure."

"You will have me utterly spoiled if I listen longer to your blandishments," he said, laughing. "Besides, the train may get tired waiting for me," he added as he walked towards the 'bus and bowed his adieu.

"Au revoir!" said the stout landlady, gayly, and retreated to her own dominion.

CHAPTER XXII.

MAXIMILIAN.

A wayfaring man acquainted with grief.—Bible.

Ten days after the departure of St. George from Walker's Hotel, a traveler on foot, with his worldly fortune in a cotton handkerchief carried on his back by a stick over the shoulder, entered the village of Riverside by the Fairmont road. He was roughly dressed, and his attire showed the ravages of wear and tear, the shoes, especially, approaching the last stage of usefulness. They evidently could not tramp many miles more without completely giving up the struggle they had been making to keep sole and body together. In these days, the man would have been called a "hobo." At that time, in that region, professional tramps were unknown, and pedestrian travelers infrequent on any of the roads. This poor fellow was apparently looking for work; and this appearance was confirmed by himself when he came along by the blacksmith shop and stopped to speak to a little group gathered to watch the smith shoe a somewhat restless horse. The blacksmith set down the horse's foot as the man approached. The manner of the wayfarer was deferential, and all looked at him as he spoke, with a slight German accent.

"Gentlemen," he said, "can any of you give a hungry man a few days' work?" Receiving no answer, he continued: "I have asked all along the road to-day from Fairmont here, but nobody had anything for me to do. It must be bad times in this part of the country."

Still receiving no answer, he asked how far it was to the next town, and was told it was ten or twelve miles. He looked appealingly from one to another. "I am very tired and hungry," he said. "I have had nothing to eat since morning and have walked a long road. Have any of you an odd job I could do to earn my supper?"

"What can you do?" asked the smith.

"Any kind of common work. I could blow the bellows or strike for you. I might shoe a horse for you, for I have taken care of horses and have put on shoes, and I can do any kind of farm work."

"What do you know about horses?" asked Jonas Blue, whose horse the smith was shoeing.

"I worked among horses a good many years," the man replied.

"Where?"

"In Cumberland, Maryland, at the Luman House stables. I was considered a good ostler, if I do say it."

Blue looked him over. He was not a promising looking candidate for favor; but then he was tired and dusty, and his dilapidated shoes gave him a vagabondish look.

"My ostler quit last night," remarked Jonas to the others. "I have a mind to give this man a trial." He would probably be glad to work for small wages. Turning to the traveler he said: "You see that sign?" pointing to the Blue Boar half a block away. The man nodded. "You go there and wait till I come. I will give you supper, and we will see if I can find any work for you."

In a quarter of an hour Blue came over leading his horse, which he hitched by the pavement. "What is your name?" he asked the man, who was sitting on the bench but rose as he approached.

"Maximilian Rudolph."

"They call you Max?"

"That is what Mr. Luman called me."

"Which Luman was that? I used to be acquainted in Cumberland."

"Samuel Luman; they called him 'Sam' because everybody liked him and made free with him."

Jonas' people had lived near Blue's Gap, in Hampshire County; and often visiting Cumberland, he well remembered Sam. Luman, who was a noted fisherman and who when the Baltimore & Ohio Railroad was first opened to the Ohio river had, with the aid of William Shriver, of Wheeling, another disciple of Walton's, transferred in the tender of an engine a lot of Ohio river black bass to the waters of the Potomac, with such success in propagation that the South Branch of the Potomac had become the finest bass stream in the United States. The man's acquaintance with Luman decided Blue to give him a job. He took him out on the back porch where were a basin, bucket of water, and a rough towel hanging on a post. "Wash and brush yourself," he said, handing Max a whisk broom. "After you have had supper I will show you the stable."

When Maximilian had washed and cleaned himself up as well as he was able, he proved to be a rather good looking man who might be twenty-eight or might be thirty-two, with a Germanic cast of face, who had a somewhat downcast, dull and listless air.

The landlord of the Blue Boar found that Max had told him no more than the truth in claiming capability in handling horses. While he seemed but a dull fellow, taking little interest in anything around him, there was no cause for complaint about the way his work was done. There was not enough about the stable to keep him employed, and he took to doing all sorts of jobs about the house, of which an industrious man finds no lack—sweeping, cleaning, looking after fires as the evenings grew cool; doing chores for the landlady; so that he was more about the house than the stable. The loungers and habitues soon came to know him. His obliging ways made him popular with them, and they would chat with him and chaff him, as occasion arose, and came to regard him as a part of the establishment before whom everything might be said that did not prejudice the hostelry.

For all his lack of interest in his surroundings, Max managed to note a good many little things that were said and done. After his work was done, he naturally sat in the back part of the bar-room and dozed the evening away, that being convenient for both him and the landlord in case any orders were to be given; but he was such a sleepy-head, that when this happened he always had to be awakened to receive them. Thus it happened that when the Esmond visitors were there at night, after the village loungers had gone, had they talked with their accustomed freedom, Max might have picked up a good many hints if he had been awake and had known what they related to. But in truth these visitors seemed to have put bits on their unruly tongues, for they had become habitually wary and careful what they said even in so safe a place as the Blue Boar bar. They seemed to have become thoroughly imbued with Harry's caution. Max had more than once been sent on errands to the Esmond place and these had been done with the same indifference as his other work.

The landlord had provided him with some whole shoes and made some other additions to his scanty wardrobe. Max did not go about the village and made no acquaintances except in the course of his work; did not go to church on Sundays and appeared to care little about his appearance. The landlady, seeing he was a rather good looking fellow, rallied him one day about his neglect of himself, and told him he ought to brush up a little and get acquainted with the girls. He replied that he had once had some experience with the gentler sex and that it had discouraged him from further attempts to gain their good graces. She concluded this might be one of the reasons for his despondency.

CHAPTER XXIII.

TURNING POLITICIAN.

All things unto all men.—St. Paul.
By the pricking of my thumbs,
Something wicked comes this way.
—Macbeth.

Well said. That was laid on with a trowel.
—As You Like It.

The Presidential Election was coming on and the country began to be stirred by meetings and orators. The box seats at the stores and shops had been moved inside and the national debate that had been carried on outside was resumed around the stoves in the evening with fresh vigor. The disappearance of the cattle-buyer and the subdued comment on the villainies of the Esmonds had given way to the greater excitement of the coming election.

A week or more before election some of the Clarksburg politicians went to Riverside by appointment to address a Democratic meeting. St. George, as a Baltimore man, had found it desirable to declare his attitude on the national issues. He had talked in the Clarksburg hotels freely, and for a man of his breeding rather loudly, about what Maryland would do in case the Black Republicans should elect and undertake to inaugurate Lincoln; that Maryland soil should never be polluted by the foot of a Yankee invader, and that he would go back home to be one of those to welcome the northern hirelings with bloody hands to hospitable graves. This kind of talk struck a chord in harmony with the dominant note in the old town, and St. George was put up a notch by the hot-heads who were pushing the Breckinridge campaign. The few Republicans there (like Ira Hart) who had been outspoken enough to be recognized as such, found it prudent to be quiet. The Bell and Everett people were mild, like their platform; and in their advocacy of "The constitution, the Union and the enforcement of the laws," did not venture to affirm that the laws should be enforced to the point of "coercion" in case such enforcement should become necessary. "Enforcement" with them was a mere figure of speech, for campaign uses.

At one of the meetings, which were held every few nights, St. George was called on, and he got up and made a red-hot speech from the extremest Southern standpoint. From this on he was looked upon as one of the drawing cards and was asked to accompany the stock speakers to various meetings at other points. This took him with them to Riverside at the time mentioned. He had ridden down with John Cassel, the lawyer, and they put up, with the rest, at the Blue Boar; and he was pleasantly greeted by the landlord, who recalled his visit with Keifer. Nothing could recommend him to mine host more than the company he was in; and yet somehow Jonas Blue was not sure that he quite liked this Baltimore man, albeit he was such a polite and agreeable gentleman. It was a case of Doctor Fell; he could not have told why, but he did not quite like him.

The sagacity of nature is beyond human finding out. Every animate creature is endowed with enough of it to know how to protect itself. In every grade of animal life the instinctive recognition of danger is proportioned to the imminence of it. Every animal liable to be made the prey of some stronger, fiercer or cunninger beast inherits an instinct that tells it what to fear and how to keep out of harm's way. Even man, when he comes to be at war with the retributive powers of society—when he has thus put himself in the category of the lower tribes—develops this animal sagacity. All the ordinary powers of apprehension, aside from reason, become sharpened, until it seems as if a new sense were added to him. The habitual criminal can scent an officer of the law as truly as the deer scents the panther lurking in ambush at the lick. Blue's instinct had given him warning. He had sniffed danger in the air but had not yet got the direction.

St. George led his own horse to the stable, remarking to the landlord that it was a horse loaned him by a Clarksburg friend who set a high value on the animal and charged him specially to see that it had proper care. When he entered the stable the ostler seemed agitated for a moment as he came forward to take the horse, but he dropped his eyes and went off to a rear stall in his usual apathetic manner. St. George followed to see the animal unharnessed, and exchanged a few words with the ostler about rubbing down and feeding. Then finding nobody was within hearing he drew nearer and a conversation in subdued tones followed for two or three minutes, and St. George walked back to the house and Max went on with his humble duties in the stable.

At the meeting after dinner, St. George was the last of the speakers. He came out strong and was hotly applauded. Harry Esmond's father, who was in the crowd and recalled St. George's visit, came forward and renewed the acquaintance and congratulated him on his speech. "That's just the kind of talk we want. I wish there was more like it." Just then John Cassell came up and shaking hands with Esmond, whom he had long known, the latter invited the two to visit the Big Elm next day (Sunday) and have dinner with him.

Cassel looked inquiringly at St. George, saying: "I am inclined to accept our old friend's invitation. What do you say?"

"Nothing could give me greater pleasure," replied St. George. "I have been there once, and that makes me wish to go again."

The old man was cordial and pressing; so it was agreed that if they stayed to the night meeting, which was talked of, they would remain over night and go to the Elm the next forenoon.

About ten next morning, which proved to be warm and bright, they rode up the lane and dismounting at the gate were met by the elder Esmond and by Harry, who walked down from the door to meet them. Harry was very cordial to both and made them feel that their visit was no intrusion. Lot Dyson and Ray Harris were standing a little distance away. Harry called them up and introduced them. St. George had seen these men, but had not been introduced, before. He had no difficulty in assigning them their place in the gang. If there was a throat to be cut, certainly Dyson was the man for the work. These were the men, he said to himself, who had slain McKinney. These thoughts flashed through one corner of his brain while he greeted the ruffians and chatted with them as politely as if they had been gentlemen he had met in some lady's drawing room.

The horses were put away and the party walked to the river and sat down under the elm. This, as the most attractive spot about the place, was the usual resort when the weather was pleasant.

St. George and Cassel admired the great tree and then the talk turned to the political outlook.

Harry confessed that for his part he was not taking a great deal of interest in the election. He had noticed that no matter how great the crisis, and how an election went, the country was always saved and things went on as usual, despite the lugubrious predictions of the politicians, smiling at St. George and Cassel. His father, he said, was taking enough interest for both and he was content to let him do it.

St. George expressed himself pretty strongly, repeating the sentiments expressed in public, speaking with confidence in regard to the feeling in Baltimore, where he knew the people so well.

Cassel's views were too well known to the Esmonds to need repeating.

St. George addressed his conversation to Harry Esmond, and sought to draw him out and win his confidence. But Esmond, while apparently open and friendly, even cordial, was not effusive; he did not volunteer any talk, nor lead the way to new topics; and St. George was obliged to admit to himself that he made no headway and was no nearer a confidential acquaintance than when he first met Esmond at Sardis.

CHAPTER XXIV.

FROM POLITICIAN TO COURTIER.

To know, to esteem, to love—and then to part.
Makes up life's tale to many a feeling heart.
—Coleridge.

While memory holds a seat
In this distracted globe—remember thee?
—Hamlet.

When they returned to the house, Loraine Esmond was on the lawn taking up some geraniums which the approach of cold weather made it necessary to remove within doors. St. George left the gentlemen and approached her. She was stooping over the plants, but arose as he came up. A rosy flush overspread her face and, retiring, left her pale, with the dark eyes and lashes darker than ever by contrast. He lifted his hat and bowed, saying, as he drew near, "Good morning, Miss Esmond."

She extended her hand. "I am glad to see you, Mr. St. George," she said simply.

"But not so glad as I am to hear you say it," he replied as he pressed her hand warmly while his eyes sought hers.

She colored at the warmth of his words. It was plain to him she had recovered in a degree from the distress she was suffering when he saw her before; but her face in repose was sad, and all semblance of pleasure, he felt, had to be forced. Yet he believed she was really pleased to meet him again.

"I wish," he said, "that we might be better acquainted."

"I could wish the same," she replied, "if circumstances were more kindly; but I fear they will not permit it."

He looked at her keenly to divine if there was any hidden meaning in her words. Her eyes dropped under his scrutiny.

"I suppose," she resumed, "you are only a casual visitor in this part of Virginia and will soon return to your Baltimore home."

"That might depend," he said. "While I have interests and strong attachments there, I am still young enough to see the whole world before me, and am not yet committed to any particular place for my life sojourn."

"Do you like our Western Virginia hills?" she asked, looking into his face.

"It is a lovely country," he said warmly, and he looked into her brown eyes as if he meant to tell her that its women were included in his praise. She understood his delicate meaning and a faint flush rose to her brow.

"I have been looking around Clarksburg in a leisurely way," he added, "to see if I could find investment for a little idle money. I think this country has a future in its great wealth of coal and timber. I am strongly attracted to your beautiful valley and to your people so far as I have had opportunities to know them. I hope these may widen and permit me to know them better."

While he spoke she looked at him in a dreamy way, hearing his words and yet apparently not following them. It was as if her thoughts were far away, revolving some problem that lay beyond this conversation and these surroundings. When he ceased, she came back to the present, and the look of sadness and repression came into her face again.

"Will you pardon my rudeness," she said, "but the dinner hour is coming on and I must go to the kitchen and help mother about the dinner. It will not do to let our guests go hungry," she added, smiling (sadly enough, he thought) as she turned to enter the house.

All St. George's favorable impressions of the girl were strengthened by this second meeting. His belief that the shadow of some terrible tragedy rested on her spirits was also confirmed. He reviewed his former thoughts and found nothing to shake his belief that McKinney had met his death within the precincts of this farm and that she was conscious of the fact; and he realized keenly the terrible position in which she was placed. Yet how could he ever hope to draw from her anything to confirm his surmises? She was not the girl to betray a family secret, even though the possession of it did rend her heart. Suppose he could win the girl's affections?

But she was not a woman to be easily won, even if she were heart-free—as to which he knew nothing.

But why let his thoughts run into such wild vagaries? He was not here to win hearts, but to break them. Yet his respect—his admiration—for this poor girl was so great he felt as if he must withdraw from a pursuit which if successful would put a rope around her brother's neck. His feelings and his duty were parting company. It was time to consider whether he would abandon the one path and take the other. For St. George was humanly tender in his finer feelings; and his compassion for this girl had been deeply touched. It is but a step from compassion to love in the case of a beautiful girl, and he felt he was in danger of opening the question whether he should take that step. This would not do. He must remember his duty and his business obligations.

After dinner the Esmonds and Mr. Cassel seemed drawn together and St. George felt free to saunter by himself around the grounds while smoking his after-dinner cigar. He threw it away when he saw Loraine come out into the lawn at the front of the house. He walked towards her and thought she did not seem displeased at his approach. The thought occurred to him that, from a strictly professional point of view, it might not be without its usefulness to allow the family to suppose that he was attracted by the daughter; at the same time he felt ashamed of such a thought in her presence.

"Miss Esmond," he said politely, "I do not know when, if ever, it will be my good fortune to visit your home again. Let me make the most of the friendly fate that finds me here today. May I not have the pleasure of a stroll by the river with you before I go?"

"I am glad to do anything you think will give you pleasure," she said, "but I fear you will find me dull company."

They walked through the gate and down to the elm and strolled some distance along the path, up the river and down again beyond the elm to a group of sycamores that sent their fantastic roots down to the water's edge, then back to the elm once more, where they stood, musing more than talking, and wrapped in dreamy reverie inspired by the loveliness around them. The frosts had done their work. The woods on the other side of the river turned their garments of russet and gold to the afternoon sun, and brown leaves rustled under their feet as they walked. The leafage of the elm, as if in its might it defied even the forces of nature, was still green, with only a delicate striping of gold around the serrated edges. All the world around them was crowned with the diadem of the most beautiful of all the seasons, and such natures as endowed this pair could not but feel the inexpressible charm of earth and sky.

They seated themselves on the rough bench under the elm.

"I have been admiring this great elm," said St. George, "as one of the things I have found here to admire, and I cannot but think what a lovely home might be made in this grand presence were other conditions of life and fortune propitious."

"This elm," said Loraine, "is a friend to whom I often come for the sense of protection and companionship it gives me. I lead a lonely life here, as you seem to have perceived, and part of the comfort I find is in communion with the natural objects around me. I often, when the weather is fine, spend the afternoon on this rough bench. Sometimes I bring a book. But books do not appeal to one among the trees, or by the river, or under the open sky. The voices of nature will not be silenced by books. The ripple of the river, the songs of birds, the sighing of the forest, the chirp of the crickets in the grass—these all distract the thoughts and steal away the attention; and one closes the book for that delightful idleness of mind that must belong to the creatures of earth and air which have no mind, which live on nature's bounty and enjoy the solace of her peace."

The girl blushed lest she had been led by her feelings to say more than was becoming.

St. George did not observe this. He was deep in thought—in admiration, it might be — either for the speaker or for her thoughts, or both.

"Books are exacting masters," he said. "They require retirement and compel us to think; and to do that we must shut out this more delightful world that appeals to the senses and to the imagination.

"Why cannot we poor mortals," he went on, "live the ideal life that nature prepares for her other creatures? Why must we alone of all her children be compelled to think and scheme, and to grind each other's bones, that we may subsist; and by our own depravity—if I may use so strong a word as describing the condition in which we are set apart from the rest of the animate world — make life a hideous thing, when it seems intended to be a dream filled with music and enchantment and the many delights to which our faculties are attuned?"

Loraine drew a sigh. "You have given expression," she said, "to thoughts that have often weighed on my spirits. When the natural world, in which man has no part, is painted in such delightful colors, why is it that all this paradise must be turned into desolation by human frailty and wrong?"

"Perhaps it is the shadow of the primal curse."

"If this is part of the divine plan," she said, "it seems a cruel one. But then our mortal vision reaches but a little way. We must believe there is beneficence beyond it all and that the evil we see, and which seems so monstrous to our apprehension, is only a necessary shadow of infinite love and compassion."

St. George brought the conversation around into more cheerful and commonplace channels, and they lingered yet an hour or two longer about the elm and along the grassy margin of the river.

"Miss Esmond," St. George said, as they walked up the lane, "if I should not have the happiness ever to see you again, you have given me an hour this afternoon which will always hold the first place among the cherished recollections of my life."

"I do not like," she replied, "to speak of never meeting again. The world is not so wide that people who like to be friends should not be able at some part of their journey to meet again. I am not without hope that in brighter hours, in some other place, under kinder fortunes, we may again see each other. I have few friends and none whom on so short acquaintance I should be so sorry to lose sight of."

He looked at her with an impulse to tell her how much he had been drawn to her—perhaps to tell her more—but her words had not evoked the warmth in her face he had expected to see bear them company. She was speaking from no warmer feeling than esteem and on that ground he met her and assured her, in most winning tones and accents, that no poor words of his could express the warm and respectful esteem she had inspired in him and what a privilege he would regard it to be held in her remembrance as worthy of her respect and friendship.

She was touched by the delicacy of his speech and showed it in the faint color that suffused her face. Her eyes filled, and she turned away to conceal the emotion she could not subdue. When the heart is sore, tears lie near the surface. A moment later she turned to him and in a low voice of exquisite feeling and modulation thanked him for his words, which she assured him would never be forgotten.

Before he left her she said to him: "We have met but twice, and yet it seems as if I had known you much longer. Perhaps this is because I see you understand me at once better than others have in years; and it is this mutual perception, coming like a flash of light, that makes our acquaintance seem so ripe."

"I confess," he said, "that I have had the same feeling. I have seen that you are wearing the crown of some terrible sorrow, and I would give years of my life——"

She turned to him with a frightened look of appeal in her deep brown eyes. "O!" she said, "do not say such things. I cannot—I dare not—listen to them. I must leave you now," she added, "and if I do not see you again before you go, bear me in your kindly remembrance."

She gave him her hand with a look he never forgot. It was appeal, gratitude—almost love—concentrated in one thrilling glance.

"As if I could ever forget you!" he said with deep emotion, as he bowed low over the hand he pressed with almost a lover's warmth.

CHAPTER XXV.

INTERVIEW WITH THE OLD WAGON MAKER

I say the tale as 'twas said to me.
—Scott.

One day, some time after the election, Jacob Holmes, the wagon maker, received a letter from Clarksburg addressed in an unknown hand. It was unusual for him to get letters from strangers; and he pondered over the envelope as he walked home, postponing the satisfaction of his curiosity and indulging all possible conjectures before opening the missive. Arrived at his shop, he sat down on his work bench, tore open the perplexing envelope and read:

"You may recall having met in August, in the stable yard of the Busy Bee Hotel, a man who was in search of Thomas McKinney, of Uniontown. I want to talk with you about that and related matters, and I think the meeting may be as much to your advantage as mine. It is not desirable for me to call on you in Riverside, but if you will come to Clarksburg and inquire for me at Walker's Hotel, I will gladly pay all the expenses of the trip and compensate you for your time. Ask for

"St. George.

"Do not mention, even to your own family, the nature of this communication or the purpose of your trip. I would like you to come, if at all, inside of three days, as I may be called away."

"I will go tomorrow," thought Holmes, after turning the letter over in his mind a few minutes. "The only time to do a thing is when you can." Besides, the letter had piqued his curiosity.

Before the midday hour the following day Mr. Holmes rode up to the Walker House and, requesting to have his horse put up, walked up to the office desk and asked Mr. Walker, who knew him, if a Mr. St. George was staying there.

"Yes," replied Mr. Walker, shaking hands with the old man, "and I think he is in his room. Perhaps you had best go up. I will show you the way."

They went up to the door, which was standing open.

"Mr. St. George," said the landlord, "here is Mr. Holmes, of Riverside, to see you. I hear," he added laughingly, "that your speech down there captured everybody and I suppose this is one of your captives."

St. George shook hands cordially with the old wagon maker and gave him a chair.

"Mr. Holmes," he began, after a pause, "I am told that you probably know a good deal of the people about Riverside who, as I believe, made way with Thomas McKinney last June. I want to be entirely frank with you and would like you to be equally open with me. I will tell you some things that must not be known to any one else and hope you will tell me some that shall also be sacredly confidential. Are you willing to meet me on this ground?"

"I am," said Holmes, "trusting you as a gentleman and man of honor."

St. George: "Your trust will not be misplaced. I am a detective from Pittsburgh, as was Mr. Bernard, whom you met. I am trying from this base of operations to get on the trail of the men who I feel sure are chargeable with McKinney's death and who got his money. I have visited Riverside and the Esmond farm twice under circumstances very favorable for giving me the confidence of Harry Esmond and his associates; but I find them keenly on their guard, and up to this time cannot see that I have made any progress towards the discovery I seek. You have lived in Riverside some years; you know these people by name, by reputation and, I understand, personally. I have heard that a son of yours is exposed to danger from them. Perhaps it may be your desire, as it is mine, to bring these villains to justice. If it is, can you tell me anything about them that will help us?"

Holmes: "I can tell you a good deal about them" (dropping his voice cautiously). "Whether I could tell you anything that would help you in this present search is another matter. Are we safe here from being overheard? Is the next room occupied?" Mr. Holmes had grown to be careful when talking of these matters.

St. George: "The next room is empty and locked up," rising and closing the door. "We can talk here in complete security."

Nevertheless, Jacob Holmes, in all he had to say in the conversation that followed, spoke in a subdued voice, sometimes little above a whisper. It was a habit of speech he had acquired.

St. George: "I do not ask you to tell me anything about your son's connection with these people further than it may serve the purpose before us."

Holmes: "I have no objection to tell you in confidence anything you want to know. My son, when we came here from Pennsylvany, was a lad scarcely of age. He fell in with these Esmonds and was a good deal at their house; sometimes worked for them about the farm. I believe he is engaged to the youngest girl—has been for a long time."

St. George started. The other did not notice it.

"She has been trying to get him to break off with them, and they, noticing he is cool and not knowing the reason, are afraid he will tell what he knows about them. He is afraid they intend to kill him for their own safety, and I'm afraid of it, too. They have not taken him into their confidence for near a year. He has been going to the house to see the girl, but has lately heard things that show him it is dangerous for him to go there."

St. George: "Where is he now?"

Holmes: "Working on the farm of one of his uncles a few miles from Riverside."

St. George: "Then he knows nothing of this taking off of McKinney?"

Holmes: "Nothing whatever. I talked with him about it after I met Mr. Bernard. He was surprised, but he said he had no doubt the man was killed up on the hill about Lot Dyson's and the body hid somewhere about the farm."

St. George: "Would they bury it?"

Holmes: "That would be too much work, and the fresh earth might be discovered."

St. George: "Would they not throw it into the river?"

Holmes: "They might, but I think not at that season of the year. If there had been a fresh in the river, they might, expecting it would be carried away. There is an old well in a thicket on the hill not far from Lot Dyson's, where a house once stood. They might throw the body in that. When George said he had no doubt they had killed him up there on the hill, he said, 'and maybe throwed him in the old well.' I expect that is the well he meant."

St. George: "Could you point out the location of that well?"

Holmes: "No; I have never seen it. I have just heard there is one there, and I know in the neighborhood of where it is. It would be dangerous to go there to look for it in daytime."

St. George: "Could it be found at night?"

Holmes: "I don't think so. After the robbery of McKee's store I went over there with my team for a load of fodder, which was in a field that borders on this thicket, and we found some of the stolen goods in one of the fodder-shocks that we pulled down. There's two or three acres of the thicket, which is very densely grown with briers and bushes; and it is somewhere in this that this well is; but I don't know what part."

St. George: "You spoke of the hill where Lot Dyson lives. Is that in the vicinity of this thicket?"

Holmes: "Yes; Dyson's house is but a few hundred yards away."

St. George: "I met Dyson at Esmonds' the day after the speaking at Riverside. Would you think he is the man to do this deed?"

Holmes: "I think so; he would do anything for money.

"Then there is another hiding-place that I know of on that farm where a body might be hid for a time. It is an old coal-bank down by the river. If they intended to put the body in the river, they would likely hide it in this coal-bank and then bring it out when the river was high and throw it in, to be carried away."

St. George: "Would not the body sink and then come to the surface later?"

Holmes: "Yes; but they would probably tie it to an old log or chunk large enough to float it."

St. George: You know where this coal-bank is?"

Holmes: "Yes."

St. George: "Could we explore that?"

Holmes: "You might; but I have reason to think it is a hiding place for stolen horses and that one or two men are liable to be found in it any time. That would make it very dangerous for a stranger to attempt to enter it."

St. George sat some time in thought. "If we could find McKinney's body," he said, "we would be justified in swearing out warrants and taking a sheriff's posse, if necessary, and arresting everybody on the place."

Holmes: "Yes, and it would take a sheriff's posse to do it."

St. George: "But how to go about the search for the body puzzles me."

Holmes: "It would be very risky. Any strangers found on that part of the farm in daytime would be liable to be shot down from cover and would not even see the person who did it. To make the search at night would not be possible."

St. George: "Do you think the landlord of the Blue Boar is in the confidence of Esmond?"

Holmes: "I have no doubt of it, for he rated George for telling things they had done and told him that if he turned state's evidence it would not screen him and would not save him from going to the penitentiary with the rest of them."

St. George: "Do you think the old man Esmond is in these things with his sons?"

Holmes: "George told me he was the worst of the lot. It was him that brought them up that way. He used to shove counterfeit money and tried to get George to take it and pass it on the shares. Of course, he is not active now, but he counsels everything."

St. George: "You spoke of the young st girl; I suppose that is the one I met there?"

Holmes: "Yes, that is Loraine—a fine girl, if she is an Esmond."

St. George: "I met only the one daughter, and I was there twice."

Holmes: "O, the other is married, to Ray Harris."

St. George: "Ray Harris! The fellow I met with Dyson there Sunday?"

Holmes: "It was forced on the poor girl. Harris knew so much they daren't refuse him, and she was compelled to take him."

Here was a new phase of the deep damnation of crime that in all his experience with its devious ways St. George had never met before. What if Loraine should be subjected to such coercion and outrage! It made his blood hot to think of it.

St. George: "You have told me a great deal, Mr. Holmes, that is interesting and may be helpful. You probably know a good deal about the history of the offenses of this crew?"

Holmes: "I could tell you a good deal about things they have done—things that George has told me; but, as I said, he does not know anything about this."

St. George: "This is all to be as a sealed book, between you and me. I may have to visit Riverside again, and if it were even known that you had called on me, the foxy landlord of the Blue Boar would scent out something suspicious. And, on the other hand, it might expose you to the fresh enmity of the gang."

Holmes: "I will not breathe it even to my own family."

St. George: "For like reasons, I think we had better not go down to dinner together. There is the risk that somebody from your village might be at the table who might mention our acquaintance where it would excite suspicion. I am greatly indebted to you for coming and for what you have told me. This" (handing him a $20 gold piece) "will be some return for your trouble and for the service you have done us."

"Do not give me a fourth of this," said Holmes, looking at the coin.

"Keep it," said St. George; "you have done us a service no one else could."

They shook hands and separated at the door of St. George's room.

CHAPTER XXVI.

RECOGNITION, DANGER, WARNING.

Out of this nettle, danger, we pluck this flower, safety. —Henry IV.

St. George continued to frequent the shady resorts of Clarksburg more from habit than from any definite expectation. One evening he met Keifer, whom he had not seen since their visit to Sardis and Esmond's. Keifer was accompanied by a dapper looking man probably under thirty, whom he introduced as "Mr. Hooker, of Pennsylvania." It was our friend who had helped along the robbery of the Riverside store, detailed in an earlier chapter. They sat down and Keifer and St. George chatted over the races and other incidents of the trip, and St. George playfully reproached him for his long absence from Clarksburg and mentioned his recent visit to Riverside and the Esmonds. Hooker took little part in the chat; seemed, in fact, rather reserved.

After they had parted from St. George, Hooker asked Keifer where he had got acquainted with him and what he knew about him.

"I met him here," said Keifer, "several months ago. He is a Baltimore man of money and is looking around here for coal lands and other investments."

"I am afraid you have been deceived," said Hooker. "This man's name is not St. George, and he is not a Baltimore man. He is a detective from Pittsburgh."

Keifer was astounded.

"I know him well," continued Hooker. "He is connected with the Duquesne Bureau, on Smithfield street. He was pointed out to me on the street by a man that knew every 'cop' and every detective in Pittsburgh; and I saw him again in Brownsville, where he was on a 'lay' for two or three months. I saw him again early in September, I think, at Uniontown. If he has been at Esmonds' twice——" he paused, for he did not know just how much Keifer might or might not know, "I should say he is a spy on some trail, and Harry ought to know it."

Keifer was overwhelmed with chagrin and rage to see how he had been overreached by St. George and quite as much over his own stupidity, for he did not question that Hooker was right. He had simply been a fool.

"Cannot you tell him?" he asked.

"I am not going back there. I am on an expedition," he said, significantly, "that takes me in another direction. But Harry ought to be posted at once."

"I'll drive down there the first thing in the morning," said the crestfallen Keifer, and they parted.

Keifer, when he got to his hotel, racked his recollection to recall the things he had told St. George about himself in their confidential exchanges, for fear there was something a detective might use against him. He could not be sure, he had been such an ass, just how much he had told and how much withheld, and the thought of it made him uneasy.

It chanced that St. George had planned a visit to Riverside for the next day. He wanted to communicate to Max some suggestions resulting from his interview with Holmes. A mile before he reached the village he overtook Keifer and rallied him for not letting him know he was coming this way. Keifer assured him he had had no thought of it when they were together the evening before, but a forgotten matter that had recurred to him made the trip necessary. They chatted the rest of the way, as St. George rode beside the buggy, and stopped at the Blue Boar. Keifer took the landlord aside and communicated his astonishing discovery regarding St. George.

Blue was excited, frightened and angry, all at once. "I knew it," he declared. "I knew there was something wrong about that man. I just felt it in my bones."

St. George had walked to the stable with his horse and been met by Max at the door. There was no one else about and they walked to the rear where Max always stalled the horse, and talked a long time in low tones.

"Will you have your horse put up?" asked Blue of Keifer.

"No, I must go right on to Esmonds', for Harry ought to know this at once. I'll stop as I come back."

He drove off and Blue, guided by an infallible instinct, hurried across lots the back way to the stable. He opened a door in the rear and silently entered the harness room, through a small opening in the partition of which he could both see and hear St. George and Max not two yards away. He listened till the conversation was concluded and St. George left the stable. His thoughts were in a tumult. While he had felt his undefined distrust of St. George, he had not till the moment of Keifer's disclosure had the faintest suspicion that Max was anything else than he appeared. He was enraged to think how cleverly this stupid tramp had taken him in. The talk between him and St. George showed plainly enough that he was a confederate, a spy set to pick up odds and ends about the stable and barroom to help the detection of—Blue knew what only too well.

When Keifer reached Esmonds' he found Harry just passing from the barn to the house. The latter was surprised to see him and said so.

"You will be more surprised by what I have to tell you," said Abe.

"Come in; it's raw out here."

They went into the sitting-room, where a soft-coal fire blazed in the grate.

"What is it?" said Esmond, impatient and always afraid of something alarming.

Keifer narrated in detail what the reader already knows regarding the statement made by Hooker as to St. George. Esmond was as much surprised as Keifer had been. "Is that possible?" he exclaimed. "Well, he's a keen one. But he didn't get anything here," he added, a moment later.

They went over the matter in all its aspects and bearings. Keifer expressed his humiliation to think he had been the means of bringing a spy to their house. Harry made him feel that he had not been in the least to blame. St. George, he said, was smooth enough to deceive the elect; and still he rather prided himself on the way he had, without intending it, held St. George off from any sort of confidence at both visits.

"Well, Abe," he said, after they had got through discussing St. George ,"I'm glad to see you. The times are pretty dull just now. Nothing in sight, is there? It may be better after while."

"Where was Hooker going?" asked Keifer.

"He's after a bank in one of the back towns. He has been setting up a job there that he thinks will be pretty fat. His partners went round by the railroad. Wanted me to take an interest in it, but I told him I was resting awhile. I'll have your horse put away and fed. You will stay till after dinner."

When Keifer came in, Loraine Esmond was in her mother's bedroom, which had a door opening into the sitting-room; the conversation between him and Harry was entirely audible to her, and her attention was quickly caught by the mention of St. George. As soon as she had gathered the purport of Keifer's communication and understood that St. George was now at the Blue Boar, she resolved to give him warning. She passed out by another door, told her mother she was going to run up to see Eloise, went to the stable and, saddling her favorite mare, "Vic," was soon galloping up the river towards the village, for she was a fearless horsewoman. Her sister's house was a few hundred yards above the mill. The ford below the dam was the shallowest. She rode through the river there and passed on up to the village on the other side. She went straight to the old stone mansion, forming her plan as she rode along. Arrived at Byers', she jumped down and hitched her horse, and was soon in the arms of "Tot."

They kissed one another, as girls will when they have no more worthy object for their caresses, and then Tot drew back and looked at Loraine inquiringly. Loraine put on an air of gayety.

"What brought you?" said Tot.

"What should bring me? I was dying to see you."

"Ah!" said the other, incredulously. "Since when?"

"Now truly I wanted to see you; I was lonesome."

"Is that all?" said Tot, who was hoping for something exciting.

"I'll tell you," said Loraine, in a confidential tone. "I was coming up to see Eloise, and as it wasn't much farther, I thought I would run over and talk with you about a new dress I'm going to have."

"Is that all?" said Tot, still doubting.

"No, that isn't all. I'll tell you the rest. Just as I was coming away, Abe Keifer came, and I heard him tell Harry that Mr. St. George had come down with him and was at the Blue Boar. Now, I want you to meet Mr. St. George, and I thought——"

"You want to see him yourself," said Tot banteringly.

"Perhaps I do," returned Loraine, "and I suspect he wants to see me." She was willing Tot should think she was smitten with the handsome Baltimorean. "So I thought you and I would run over and see

Jen, and maybe while there we might run across him."

"That will be delightful," said Tot. "Wait till I get my hat on."

A few minutes later the girls were on their way to visit the landlady of the Blue Boar, chattering as if neither had ever known the shadow of a care. When they entered the hall of the hotel by the side door, they came face to face with Mr. St. George, who, overcoat on arm, was about entering the parlor. He was both surprised and pleased at the encounter. Loraine and he shook hands cordially and she, turning to Tot, presented her. St. George responded gracefully to the introduction and they sat down in the parlor and chatted pleasantly for a few minutes, when, at an invisible sign from Loraine, Tot arose and excused herself to run in and greet the landlady.

The manner of Loraine underwent an instant change. She arose and drew near St. George and said in a low, impressive tone: "I have just come from home to tell you that your life is in peril here and that you must go away at once. I only learned this within an hour and lost not a moment."

Astonished at her words, St. George hesitated.

"I cannot explain," she said. "Do not ask it. Only trust me. Get your horse and go at once."

"I cannot leave you in this abrupt way," he said.

"You must, if you care for your life or my regard."

He looked a moment into her serious eyes and saw there the grave solicitude expressed in her words.

"I would not come to tell you this," she said, "if the danger were not real and imminent."

He was convinced and, extending his hand, in which she placed her own, he said, with deep feeling and a warm pressure of the hand:

"Then, if I must go, farewell, and God bless you."

He passed out of the street door, walked to the stable and met Max at the door. "Give me my horse," he said. The horse was standing in the stall with saddle and bridle on, needing nothing but to tighten the girths. A minute later St. George was in the saddle, Max standing at the horse's bit. "I have just been warned," said St. George, "that my life is in danger here. Some discovery has been made. Of course, they do not connect you with me in any way, but be on your guard." He rode away, passed over the bridge and out of the village.

Loraine sat thoughtful two or three minutes after St. George had left her; then she walked to the street door and, looking towards the stable, saw him mount and ride off. She passed into the dining-room, where she found Tot and the landlady chattering like canaries and as gay.

"O," she said to Tot, "I didn't have but a minute with him after all. 'Business!' Tot, don't ever marry a man of business; if you do, you'll have to take second place in his affections."

"Ah," said the landlady, "I hear St. George has been down to see you twice."

"No, certainly not more than once, for when he came first he did not know I was there. But this is three times he has come to see somebody at the Blue Boar," and she looked mischievously towards the youthful and good-looking landlady.

"I don't believe he comes to see any of us," she said. "It is somebody's cattle farm, or timber tract, or coal lands. That's the kind of rivals that cut us out."

"Don't you believe it," said Tot. "And now that I've been introduced to him, I am going to set my cap for him. They say he's rich, and we know he is handsome."

"But," said the landlady, looking at Loraine, "if this is to be a scramble between you and Tot, what is to become of the George who isn't a saint?"

"O, he'll be one some time. But saints don't grow on every bush."

"All the more reason why I should pluck this one," laughed Tot.

And thus they rattled on, Loraine as gay as the others, and really light-hearted for the moment over the success of her mission to St. George.

The girls returned to the stone mansion, and Loraine, asking Tot to come and see her just as soon as she could, mounted her horse.

"What about that new dress?" asked Tot, standing by the gate.

"I'll tell you when you come to see me," laughed Loraine as she rode away.

Keifer came back to the Blue Boar about the middle of the afternoon and was surprised to learn that St. George had abruptly returned to Clarksburg. "This is odd," he remarked. "He didn't get away any too soon," said Blue.

Next day the landlord received a note from St. George enclosing money for his score and explaining that a messenger had brought him word that obliged him to return to Clarksburg at once. "I did not see any messenger," thought Jonas, "but he may have come while I was at the blacksmith shop." He went to the stable and asked Max if somebody had come for St. George. Max, taking the cue, replied that a boy had brought a note and ridden away and that St. George had gone directly after. "Then he will be back again," thought Blue, "and we will have a chance to settle with him."

CHAPTER XXVII.

SURPRISE.

Can such things be
And overcome us like a summer cloud?
—Macbeth

The evening of the second day after Keifer's visit to him, Harry Esmond dropped into the Blue Boar. He had spent the earlier part of the evening at the stone mansion, not caring to call on Blue till the day's business was over and the loungers gone home. There was no fire in the den, and Jonas took him into the bar-room, and they sat behind the high counter, out of sight even if any one had looked in at the windows. Blue had sent Max to bed, telling him he would not be wanted again that night.

The two sat down and looked at each other a few moments as men do who have encountered some matter of mutual astonishment, as much as to say, "Did you ever?"

"Well, don't that beat the dickens?" began Jonas, who was not given to plain, ordinary swearing.

"It beats the devil and his imps," returned Harry, with emphasis.

"It may beat the devil, but not his imps, for we were not taken in by it," laughed Jonas.

"But would have been if we hadn't all been watching our p's and q's," returned Esmond. "I think from what Keifer said the other day, he was off his guard and told St. George some things he wishes now he had kept to himself. St. George would do well to beware of Keifer, for he is furious and will settle the account if he gets a chance."

"Wouldn't blame him," said Blue. "I want to tell you," he went on, "when Abe stopped here the other day with St. George he took me to one side and told me what Hooker had told him. I came back to the street door and saw St. George leading his horse to the stable. All at once it struck me as peculiar he should always want to go to the stable to see after his horse, and the thought flashed into my mind whether he did not go to see Max. I'd never have thought such a thing if it hadn't been for what Abe had told me. So I ran around the other way and went into the stable at the south end door, which opens in the harness and feed room, and there, not two yards away, stood St. George and Max in close confab, and through a knothole I could see them and hear everything they said. St. George asked Max if he had made any discoveries. Max said nothing of importance. Had he been over to your place again? No. Had you been about the Blue Boar? No. Then St. George told him he had learned there was an old well in a thicket on the hill near Dyson's house and there was reason to believe the body had been thrown in that well, and he wondered if Max could not go across there some day rabbit hunting and see if he could locate that well."

Harry sat with open eyes, amazed. "How do you suppose," he said, "St. George ever got hold of that? Did he see anybody here the day he spoke who could have told him anything?"

Blue: "I don't think so, because he was about the house all the time with the Clarksburg men who came with him, except when he was speaking and until he and Cassel started down to your house."

Esmond: "Was old Jake Holmes about here that day?"

Blue: "I saw him in the back part of the crowd while the speaking was going on; but he did not come near the house and I am sure he was not near St. George. I am sure they don't know one another at all. The old man doesn't come about the house any more since I gave George that raking."

Harry was thoughtful. "I wonder who could have told him. It seems he found out some things after all. I can't imagine where he got it. This Max has never been over there?"

Blue: "I sent him over to your house twice, but I am certain he went and came straight back. He was not gone long enough for an excursion on the hill. And what should he know at that time to make him want to go there? He didn't know about this till St. George told him the other day."

"O, that's true; I forgot. I will post Lot about this, and if Mr. Max or anybody else goes rabbit hunting around that thicket, he will run against somebody after larger game. Who is this Max? Where did he come from?"

Blue: "He came tramping through the town last fall one evening and stopped at the blacksmith shop to ask for work—the most distressed, miserable looking cuss you ever saw. He hadn't a whole garment to his back and his shoes were just letting his feet out on the ground. I was there getting the shoes changed on Sam. I asked the poor devil some questions, and he told me he was from Cumberland and had worked in the Luman House stables for Sam Luman. You know I used to be acquainted in Cumberland and knew Sam Luman. Well, his story seemed so plausible—and Bob had just quit—that I took him in."

Esmond: "I'd have done the same. Don't it beat the devil how these fellows fix up a story. It seems hard to believe that stupid fellow is a detective. He came from Cumberland, you know, where you came from," laughing.

"Yes, and St. George came from Baltimore," said Jonas, turning the laugh.

"That's a fact," said Harry. "They always hail from some unexpected quarter. That's their business. Well," he resumed, "what do you think we ought to do with Max? He does not know we suspect him."

"What ought to be done with St. George?"

"Since he is anxious to find McKinney, perhaps we had better send him the same road."

Blue: "He went away very suddenly the other day after Abe had gone to your house; but next day I got a note from him sending me the money for feeding his horse and saying a boy had followed him from Clarksburg with a message that required him to go right back. His going away seemed to me so queer that I asked Max and he told me a boy rode up with a letter for St. George and went right away again, and St. George came down and took his horse and went off. It must have been while I was over at the blacksmith shop. It shows he does not know that we are on to him and he will be back again."

Esmond: "Then we had better let Max alone for the present and keep quiet till St. George comes back. Meanwhile we'll consider what ought to be done."

CHAPTER XXVIII.

DEFEAT.

'Tis not in mortals to command success,
But we'll deserve it.

—Addison's Cato.

The night after St. George's return to Clarksburg he sat down in his room to go over the developments and progress—want of progress, he felt—in the matter of his pursuit of the murderers of Thomas McKinney. He had arrived at the point where Bernard had left off: he was known to them as a spy. This was the end of his usefulness on that line of attack. The danger this exposed him to did not specially concern him, because that was incident to the pursuit. He had yielded to Loraine's entreaties to quit the Blue Boar abruptly because he realized the sacrifice she had made, and the feeling that prompted it, when she came to warn him, and he wanted to relieve her mind at the earliest moment.

He went back to see if he could account for her warning. What had occurred since his last visit to the great elm, when he felt sure there was not a breath of suspicion? First, his interview with Holmes. Could the old man have incautiously let out anything that had been carried to the Blue Boar or the Esmonds? He did not believe it. What else? His meeting with Keifer and Hooker. Then there was Keifer's visit to Esmonds' the next day, which Keifer had not mentioned the night before. In this connection it occurred to him Loraine had said in the Blue Boar parlor she had learned of his danger only within an hour. That would have been coincidently with Keifer's arrival at their house. Then Keifer had gone there to tell Esmond of some suspicion or discovery. But what? Hooker! Who was Hooker, anyhow? From Pennsylvania—western Pennsylvania, it was fair to assume. Could Hooker have known him? Had he ever seen Hooker before? He had a trained memory for the faces of criminals and thought he could recognize any face he had ever seen in the rogues' gallery. Hooker must be a criminal or he would not consort with Keifer; but he could not remember that he had ever seen the man. But Hooker must have known and recognized him. That must be the explanation. Hooker had recognized him as a detective; had told Keifer, who had gone straight to Esmond. Loraine had perhaps overheard Keifer's communication and had come straight to the Blue Boar to tell him —what she saw was the logical consequence—that he was in peril. This was the goal his thoughts had reached, and the reader knows how near he was to the truth. His heart warmed towards the girl when he thought of what she had done for him, and it gave him a pang to remember what old Mr. Holmes had told him—that she was not heart-free.

He was at the end of his detective tether. Now, could he venture to call on the civil authorities of Harrison county and demand that the sheriff take a posse and arrest Esmond and his connections? This was too important a step to be taken unadvisedly. He wrote to Bernard, detailing the situation and concluding with the question he had just asked himself. In four days came the reply: "Have you evidence strong enough to support you in swearing out the warrant? Be sure of this before acting."

He went over to the office of Squire Werninger, an old and experienced magistrate, with whom he had made some acquaintance, and with him went over the facts point by point. What evidence was there that would stand the analysis of the courts, asked the magistrate? What could be proven? He could prove that a man answering the description of McKinney had visited Riverside at a certain date; had crossed the river on the ferry and had turned from the ferry into the road leading down the river past the Esmond farm. What more? Nothing tangible. After that there was nothing but inference and deduction. entirely convincing to St. George but not worth presentation as evidence in court. Of what value when judicially analyzed would be his inferences based on the distress of Loraine Esmond, or the statements made by Holmes and others regarding the reputation of these people? How could he prove that McKinney had not turned off at the road leading to Maston's, or that leading up to Dietrich's, before reaching the Esmond homestead, or that he had not passed on beyond it?

It would not do. He could not make the oath necessary to warrant the magistrate in issuing so important a process or produce evidence to support it if issued. He was obliged to report to Bernard that no evidence strong enough to warrant an arrest had been obtained. His thoughts reverted to Max. He being wholly unsuspected, might yet pick up a clue that would open the way to what seemed the unassailable security of the murderers.

A few nights later he met Keifer again in one of the gambling resorts he still went to, and Tarbert with him. They affected to meet him with the former show of pleasure and Keifer was even effusive in his familiarity; but St. George knowing what he did, and what they did not suppose he knew, easily saw through the pretense. He, too, affected to be unconscious of any change, and they soon left him, mentioning an engagement as the excuse.

He loitered away the evening watching the play and, tired at last, started to return to his hotel. It was near midnight, bright moonlight, the streets deserted. Clarksburg at that time was not the metropolis it deems itself now. Honest people then went to bed with the chickens; few strangers came and went, and no such thing as a policeman, night or day, had then been thought of. In this peaceful old rural town it had never occurred to St. George to be afraid of anything save the wiles of its pretty girls, and he had been coming and going at all hours of night without thought of danger. He turned into Pike street while yet a long way from his hotel and walked past several open lots along a neglected hedge that ended at an alley. He had got perhaps ten paces beyond this alley when the sharp crack of a firearm, accompanied by the "ping" of a bullet, saluted his ear. He was startled, for the ball came so close he felt it fan his cheek. He turned and looked back. No one was in sight. Turning again to walk on, another report and another bullet which he felt strike his hat warned him that he must get away. It was no use to stand there to be shot at by an unseen assassin, he himself without a weapon. He sprang forward and ran for a block, and then, walking briskly the rest of the way, was soon at the hotel. The office was still open, the porter asleep in his chair, and, taking down his key, he went to his room, took off his hat and looked at it. The bullet had passed through the crown so low it must almost have grazed the scalp. When the first shot was fired, he had supposed the object was robbery; but at the second he thought of Keifer and Tarbert and he felt an instant conviction they were his assailants. He now had no doubt of this. He recalled the shot that had been fired at Bernard and realized that he had to do with a set of thugs against whom there was no safety anywhere. He now understood, better than before, Loraine's urgency that he should leave the Blue Boar without delay. She had known the methods of the gang better than he.

He did not mention his adventure next morning. There were good business reasons why he should avoid the notoriety it would provoke, and he cared nothing for it except as it bore on his mission. He knew how vain would be any attempt to discover the assassins or prove anything against them, sure as he was himself of their identity.

Two days later he had a letter from Bernard, requesting him to return to Pittsburg, as his usefulness here was clearly at an end.

St. George was of the same opinion. He put the mutilated hat in his trunk to show his associates in the Pittsburg office as a sort of object lesson to illustrate the story he would have to tell, and that evening quietly bade good-bye to the Walker and to some associations that had been pleasant to him and to others.

CHAPTER XXIX.

VANISHMENT.

—These our actors.
As I foretold you, were all spirits, and
Are melted into air, into thin air.
—Tempest.

Ten days after St. George's departure from Clarksburg, a letter for Mr. Maximilian Rudolph arrived at the Riverside post-office. The postmaster knew who Maximilian was, and as he had never asked for a letter and probably never would, he obligingly took it to him at the Blue Boar stable.

Max looked at the superscription and then at the postmark, and his face brightened. "O," he said, "that's from an old crony I used to work with at the Luman House. I know his writing. I'm fery much oblige to you." He walked to the rear of the stable and opened and read the letter. What was in it nobody in Riverside ever knew.

Max was around the house and stable till after dark; but when it came time to fix up the fires for the night he was nowhere to be found; nor was he ever seen again by the landlord of the Blue Boar or by anybody else in the village.

His disappearance was matter for a good deal of conjecture among the habitues of the house. The postmaster, who recalled Max's remark, was of opinion that he had experienced a sudden attack of homesickness, or that his old friend had made him some very enticing offer, and perhaps enclosed him money to travel on; for Max had not drawn any pay in cash and could not be in possession of a cent. When people asked Blue what had become of him, his reply was that he guessed he had "gone back to Cumberland to eat his Christmas dinner." But secretly he was more puzzled than any of the rest and for different reasons. Had somebody warned Max that he was in danger? And if so, who?

CHAPTER XXX.

INDEPENDENT ENTERPRISE.

Enterprises of great pith and moment.
—Hamlet.

The deep damnation of his taking off.
—Macbeth.

Christmas came, as it does every year, and brought around the accustomed turkey. Thanks to Loraine's assiduous care, there was at the Big Elm a fine flock of the national bird and it had contributed a brace of big gobblers for the Christmas dinner. It had been a prosperous year for the Esmonds and they were all to gather at the family board for a reunion, at which matters of general concern could be discussed along with the turkeys. Lot Dyson and his wife, Ray Harris and his, Guy Esmond and his, and Lynn Johnson, who did not have any, joined the family in the season's cheer. Not fifteen minutes before the call to dinner, who should ride up to the gate but Hooker. He dismounted and came in, accompanied by one of the younger boys. All were surprised except Harry, who knew Hooker would return this way from his expedition. He was warmly welcomed all round and was himself in high spirits; and the dinner table was a very cheerful one for all save Loraine, who had lost the habit of cheerfulness and found it hard to regain. Johnson looked a little saturnine and snaky, for he was getting dreadfully short, and Dyson looked hungry, as he always did; but the royal feast brightened even his wolfish countenance.

Hooker's horse was taken to the barn, and after dinner the men walked out to look at it, for they were connoisseurs in horseflesh and looked at horses much as the dilettanti look at pictures.

"It's a horse I hired at the Bartlett livery, in Clarksburg," explained Hooker, "and I promised to send him back by mail carrier tomorrow."

"Why send him back at all?" suggested Harris; "he's good for $75."

"He is not worth the trouble," said Hooker. "Besides, I'm not after any small game these days. I don't need to be. Look here, boys!"

He thrust his hand into his trousers pocket and drew out a roll of bank notes as thick as his wrist. He spread them open in the palm of one hand and turned them over, face up, one by one. There were fifties and hundreds by the dozen; nothing less than $20.

"W-h-e-w!" whistled Johnson, whose snaky eye glittered at the sight; "you are well fixed, for a fact!"

Harry, who alone knew where the money came from, was surprised at the size of the spoil. Hooker, whose head was turned by his good luck and the surprise he excited, continued: "That's only a part of it," pulling out a bursting pocketbook from the other pocket and holding it up without opening it.

"You struck it rich," said Harry.

"You bet I did!" Hooker was so inflated he could not conceal his exultation. He did not dream there could be any danger in making such a display among friends. But even wolves when ravenous have been known to devour one another, and the leaders in the French Terror guillotined each other as fast as it stood them in hand to do so. If Hooker had known the views held by Dyson and Johnson in the matter of being led into temptation, he would have been more discreet.

"Put up your money," said Harry, laughing; "you make us feel poor, and that is not pleasant for Christmas time."

It seemed to occur to Hooker that he had been foolish, and he turned the talk into other channels.

"What are your plans?" asked Harry. "Will you stay with us over the holidays?"

"I cannot," replied Hooker. "I must go on down the river tomorrow night."

"Shall we send your horse up to Jonas tonight to go by the mail carrier in the morning?"

"If one of the boys will take him, here is a dollar for his trouble. How am I to get towards home?"

"Is that last horse Tarbert sent down still in the barn?" Harry asked.

"Yes," replied Ray, "and I'm getting tired of feeding him."

"That will just fit, Hooker; you can pass him on to market and account to us as usual."

They went back to the house, and while the mother and daughters and Mrs. Dyson busied themselves about the dining-room and kitchen, the "men folks" got together and held a confidential session over everything of recent occurrence that concerned them collectively.

Harry expressed his satisfaction over the cue that Hooker had given Keifer about St. George and then told Hooker about Blue's discovery that his tramp hostler, who came to him two or three months ago, was a confederate of St. George's. These matters were intensely interesting to the whole crew. In the course of the talk Harry related what Blue had overhead St. George say to Max about the old well. All pricked up their ears at this.

"How do you suppose he got on to that?" growled Lot.

"Some traitor. Do you think it could be George?" asked Johnson.

"Who knows where George is?" Johnson continued.

"He's working at his Uncle Andy's," answered Ray, "and I have it straight that he has not been off the farm since he went there. How should he know anything about St. George or St. George know anything about him?"

"That's so," remarked Harry. "'Jone' knows just where St. George was, and who he saw, each time he was at the Blue Boar. I'm puzzled to think how he got hold of that."

"Well, let me tell ye," quoth Lot, savagely, "they'd better not monkey around that thicket or there will be some more of them in the old well before they know it."

After supper Lot, Ray and Guy prepared to go home. "Come and stay with us tonight, Lynn," said Lot, and his wife seconded the invitation.

"Better stay here," said Mrs. Esmond; "we will find a place for you to sleep."

"I will go with Lot tonight, to keep him from being afraid of the old well," said Johnson, with a grimace, and a few minutes later they went.

Dyson and Johnson sat before the fire talking in low tones long after Mrs. Dyson had gone to bed. They seemed to find the talk deeply interesting and their conclusions harmonious and satisfactory. As they were about to separate for the night Dyson remarked: "You remember the time we divided the McKee goods upstairs here, and what a hog he was, and how he took at least double his fair share? I said to myself then that we'd get even with him some time."

"And we will," replied Johnson, "sure's you live."

The "barn" referred to in the previous day's conversation, where the horse for Hooker was in keeping, was a place of concealment that will be described in a later chapter, a quarter of a mile or more up the river from the homestead.

Next evening Harry Esmond had an engagement in the village, so after supper he bade good-bye to Hooker and set out to walk over. A little after dark Hooker made his adieus to the family and walked up to the "barn" where he understood he would find Dyson or Lynn, who would have the horse in readiness for him, and he would then ride directly down the river without stopping again at the house. Ten to fifteen minutes later a horseman rode rapidly down the road past the elm.

"There goes Hooker!" said one of the younger boys, who was standing at the front door listening to hear him go by; "and he's going just like the old Nick was after him."

Next morning a stray horse was found wandering about the streets of Worthlesston. The reins were on his neck and there were stains on the saddle that looked suspiciously like blood. He was discovered by the clerk who came early to open Millen's store and was put in the stable, where a great many who had heard of the find went during the day to see if they knew the animal. Nobody there had ever seen it before. There was a world of conjecture about the tragedy that appeared to connect itself with the turning of the horse at large, but no owner ever appeared, and as nobody in that region was missing, the conclusion was that some stranger passing through in the night had been murdered for his money. The horse was finally sold as an estray and the excitement died out.

The Esmonds were not long in hearing of the horse and Ray Harris went down to see it. He recognized it instantly as the animal that had been ridden away by Hooker, but gave no sign. The Esmonds were greatly puzzled. They had no doubt Hooker had been robbed and murdered somewhere about Worthlesston, but how had it happened? They could not help feeling a shade of envy that anybody should have got such a prize without their having a share. Hooker never reached home, nor was ever heard of.

A few days later, when another disappearance was exciting conjecture in the village, an old blacksmith living at the eastern border of the town recalled that he had one night, not long after dark, heard, or thought he heard, in the direction of the Lot Dyson hill, the cry of a man in mortal agony. It was only a single scream, and he thought it possible he had been mistaken.

CHAPTER XXXI.

DISAPPEARANCE.

Farewell! a word that must be and hath been—
A sound which makes us linger;—yet—farewell.
—Byron.

Time sped. The seasons rolled through the beautiful Autumn into the arms of the pitiless Winter. The cold set in early and held on stiffly till the holidays. Then came a change; and a January thaw, with its downpours of rain, its flood and mud, followed directly after the opening of the new and momentous year. The streams came up with a rush to almost unprecedented heights for a winter flood. The ice went out with rather more than the usual disasters to the timbermen whose rafts had been caught in the river by the early freeze-up and the absence of a fall freshet. But in a day or two the river was nearly clear of ice, though still at flood-tide.

George Holmes did not come home till some days after New Year's. The family were rejoiced to welcome him and he was unaffectedly glad to be once more at home. The night after his return he wrote his letter to Loraine and got his sister, who was on visiting terms at the Esmond homestead, to undertake to carry it to her next morning.

"Be sure," he said, "not to let anyone but Loraine see this or know anything about it. If she is not at home, don't leave it for her. Unless you can put it in her own hand, bring it back."

She promised to faithfully follow his directions, and the next afternoon came back and said she had delivered the letter to Loraine herself.

"Did she say anything to you about it?" he asked.

"No, but I found her crying a little while after, and I think it was about something in the letter. And then afterward she seemed glad and cheerful, as if she had got over it."

This is the letter that he had sent her:

"January 6th.

"My Darling:

"I am going away now at the first hour I can find the means. Don't be scared when you hear I have disappeared, for I shall not let a soul here know of my purpose. Til. does not know what is in this letter. Breathe not a word of it to a living person. I have put off the old life and the old weakness and see now with clear eyes. I am a new man from this hour with the one purpose put into my heart by your words. I can wait, and you can. If life is spared me, time shall bring us together again when I shall be worthy of you. Trust me and wait for me. George."

In the dusk of the evening he put on his overcoat, for it was chilly, and walked down to look at the river, picking his way along the ferry road to the water's edge, where the boats lay. The river was still at flood stage, but nearly clear of ice and drift. He stood and looked at the darkening stream a long time in deep reverie. "It is hard to go away without seeing her once more," he thought, "though it seems best." He saw, while hardly conscious of it, another skiff near the one he recognized as the ferryman's. As his reverie passed, it occurred to him that this was what he was looking for. He stepped nearer and looked at it closely in the fading light. He recognized the boat as belonging to Raleigh Johnson. It was chained to a ring in the ferry-road timber, but he noticed it was not locked. He stepped into it and found it dry and in good condition and oars in the row-locks. He stood musing. What was he thinking of? "It looks as if this was left unlocked just for me," was what he was saying to himself. "Why not after all?" His ear caught a step as of some one coming down to the ferry. He could not in the gathering darkness see the person who was approaching; but he undid the chain and, laying it softly in the boat, shoved it off the shore and, taking the oars, rowed quickly into the gloom that now enveloped the river.

The ferryman had gone down to see that his boats should not be left aground by the fall in the river. He pushed them out and propped them a little way off shore. Then he noticed that Johnson's skiff, which had been there an hour before, was gone, and he recalled the fancy that he had heard the dip of oars just before he got down to the river. He listened and peered into the darkness, but he saw nothing nor heard anything save the eddying waters and their low ripple as they rolled their way onward to the sea.

CHAPTER XXXII.

MYSTERY.

Pluck out the heart of my mystery.
—Shakespeare.

When bed-time came for the Holmes family the evening after George had left the house and had not come in, they were uneasy, though not alarmed; for they concluded he had gone to Esmonds' to see Loraine. Let Jacob Holmes tell this part of his story in his own words as they lie before me:

"Next morning—Tuesday morning, as near as I can recollect—between the hours of eight and nine o'clock, young Nick Esmond came into my shop inquiring for a gun that George had fetched there some weeks before. I says to him: 'There is a gun up in the house; I don't know whose it is.' I went up into the house with him, got the gun and handed it to him. He appeared to be in a great hurry.

"My family asked him: 'Nick, did you see anything of George? Or do you know anything about him?'

"He said he did not. He went down to the shop and I asked him the same question myself, thinking that he didn't just like to say before the family where he was and that he would tell me. But he said that he did not know; that he had not saw him.

"A week elapsed until Sunday. Sunday morning, I was seated by my fire when my wife got up before day. She exclaimed, says she: 'Jake, you must go and see about George.' I says to her: 'Get breakfast and I will go down to Prim's (the cabin across the river from the elm) and I will holler over and see if I can hear anything of him.'

"I went there and called three or four times. At last I saw Mrs. Esmond coming from the direction of the old stable with a tin bucket in her hand; and I called her; but the more I called the more she hurried and made me no answer and went into the house.

"I then saw young Nick coming in the same direction. I called him and he answered me. I requested him to come down to me (to the bank of the river), I wanted to see him. When he came down I asked him did he know anything about George? He answered he did not unless he was at Tom Wilmoth's.

"Said I: 'Nick, did he tell you he was going to Tom Wilmoth's?'

" 'Yes,' in an easy tone; but at the same time he spoke and said, says he: 'I will go to Tom Wilmoth's and I will see and let you know.'

"I said: 'Well, Nick, go to-day and let me know. I feel uneasy about him.'

"Nick never came near my house; but on Monday evening my little boy John told me he heard Nick Esmond tell Jim that George was at Tom Wilmoth's. I do not know that I made any inquiry of the boy at that time; but after a little Jim come in and I asked Jim what Nick had told him. Jim said that Nick had said that he had started to go to Tom Wilmoth's but had met John Harvestry and Maria going up home, and they had told him George was at Tom Wilmoth's. I told Jim I did not believe a word of it.

"The next morning I got a horse and went down to Wilmoth's, and learned that George was not there and had not been since the time he left home.

"I came on home, when I learned of the family that old Mrs. Johnson had been there and had told about their boat being missing. I go down here to Jonas Blue's and there find Raleigh Johnson. I said to him that it appeared their boat was missing. He asked me: 'What about the boat?' I said their boat was missing, and George was missing, and I did not know what to make of it. He replied that there was no danger of his being drowned, of course.

"I started out from Jonas Blue's to go up home, and saw Ray Harris and Nick Esmond coming towards Blue's. When I got here by Store's blacksmith shop, Nick Esmond came running over to me.

"'Uncle Jake, George is at Tom Wilmoth's.'

"Says I: 'Nick, there's not a word of truth in it.'

"He asked me, in a kind of passion as it were, how did I know?

"Says I: 'I know by going to see.'

"He then: 'Where do you think,' he says, 'George is?'

"Says I: 'Nick, I fear that George is not on the land of the living.'

"When I said that his color left him and he became pale.

"'O,' he says, 'there is no danger. George is not drowned,' said he, 'for he had a good boat to go over in and he was a good swimmer.'

"On Friday, the day before the speaking of Lewis and Carlile in Riverside, I went over the river to Jacob Fontrey's. When I returned to the skiff, which was the ferryman's, here was Granny Pugh, waiting, as I supposed, that she could go over the river. We got into the skiff and came over the river; and as we landed, or about the time of my tying the skiff, she says to me:

"'I suppose you have heard from George?'

"I says: 'No, we have not.'

"'Why, la me, we heard you had got a letter from him and he was in Pennsylvania.' Says she. 'I was over at Guy's and I heard Guy tell his father that George had gone to Wheeling to enlist.'

"I asked her where he got that information.

"She said she didn't know unless it was at Worthlesston or Fairmont. It was the same day Guy went down to get that horse that had been stolen from Titchenell's. Says she:

"'He will be over here tomorrow at the speaking, and you can see him and he will tell you all about it.'

"I went in the forenoon and found Guy standing on Jonas Blue's porch. I went to him and asked him, says I:

"Where did you get this report that George had gone to Wheeling to enlist?'

"'Well,' says he, 'down in Worthlesston.'

" 'Well, who did you hear speak about it?'

"He didn't know; he believed it was Enoch May.

"Says I: 'Old Enoch May? I do not know him.'

" 'It is Hence's son, a truthful and credible boy,' says he.

" 'But, says he, 'I am going down tomorrow and I will let you know all about it.'

"He was to let me know on Monday. 'Very well,' said I. Monday came and I went down and he was standing on the out-porch in front of the house.

" 'Well,' said I, 'Guy, this rumor concerning George?'

" 'O,' he says, 'it is to Pittsburgh.'

"Well, on Tuesday I went to Worthlesston and hunted up May and asked him how did he get the information that George had gone to Wheeling or Pittsburgh to enlist? Guy Esmond had told him so the time he was down getting that horse he had taken from Titchenell's.' "

Somewhere about this time, the wife of a physician named Irman, living in property adjoining the Blue Boar tavern, was one evening in an out-building that stood against the rear of the Blue Boar smoke-house. The board-walls of both buildings were sufficiently open of joint to allow conversation on one side to be plainly heard on the other.

The landlord and his wife were in the smoke-house. He was telling her of somebody that had been killed—or was to be, she could not make out which, not having heard the beginning of the conversation. But she heard him say it was "because he was known to all this burglary;" they had become "afraid he would turn State's evidence and send us all to the penitentiary."

His wife asked: "What do you mean when you say 'burglary'?"

"Why," he replied, "this stealing of goods and horses, and all this that was done;" and they had "thought it best to put him out of the road."

She asked him: "Had you any hand in this business?"

"No," he replied, "but I am known to it all."

Mrs. Irman, knowing of George Holmes' disappearance, and also of his relations to the Esmonds and of theirs to the landlord of the Blue Boar—all of which was notorious to everybody in the village —did not doubt the conversation related to him. She became frightened and ran to the house, afraid to hear more, for she realized it was a dangerous secret. She told some family friends, who advised her to keep her own counsel; but some hint of the matter leaked out, and it preyed on her so that she kept the door locked when her husband was out, and finally left the village and went to friends at Fairmont. It was given out by somebody in the village that she was "crazy." In an interview Jacob Holmes had with her February 27th at Fairmont, Mrs. Irman made these statements, which were confirmed by her husband as having been made to him at the time. "All but the crazy," she said; "I was only afraid."

It soon became widely known that young Holmes had disappeared. Knowing all the things he did pointing to a tragedy, the poor old man felt there could be no doubt as to the fate that had overtaken his boy. But he was powerless to bring the slayers to justice. While a great deal of interest—even excitement—was felt in the community when all the suspicious circumstances became known, nobody offered any practical help; and public excitement over the approaching election for members of the Richmond convention, the issue of which all felt would be secession and war, overshadowed any mere matter of local crime and personal bereavement however distressing.

CHAPTER XXXIII.

DISINTEGRATION.

Fold their tents, like the Arabs,
And as silently steal away.

—Longfellow.

Events were thickening. Clouds on the national horizon were darkening. The Convention at Richmond had met; and while the loudest voice was for "the Union," it was accompanied by qualifications. All felt the crisis in the air. There was through all the land an ominous rumbling like the forerunner of an earthquake. Matters of local concern that would have been ordinarily provocative of the keenest interest took secondary place at the evening gatherings in shops and stores or on the street corners where groups assembled. Yet the minor tragedies of life, like the one we are following, went on their several courses, despite the overshadowing tragedy preparing for the nation.

Disintegration among the bandits had set in. They were not only feeling the general disturbance but special reasons had transpired promotive of a break-up. For the first time in the history of the gang two of its subordinate but indispensable members felt themselves able to go away and take care of themselves. A few days after the disappearance of Holmes, Lynn Johnson got out his horse and set off up the river. He told Harry Esmond he had been thinking for some time of making a trip into one of the upper counties to see if some better opportunities could not be found there for an honest citizen to make his living. He thought he would be able to persuade Tarbert to go with him, and expressed the belief that this was a good locality to be away from for a while.

Harry acknowledged that he also had been looking forward to a time when this part of the country would be too hot to hold them. Perhaps that time was not so far away. "Keep me advised where you are. May be you will see more of us before a great while."

Next day Dyson mentioned to the elder Esmond that he had thought some of moving up on Bingamon this spring, where he had heard of a place he could rent on the shares to good advantage.

"Why, Lot," said Mr. Esmond, "what do you want to go away for? You can make more money, and make it easier, than by farming."

"Well, you know, Uncle Nickie," replies Lot, with his grim smile, "a change of pasture is sometimes good for sheep."

Esmond mentioned the matter to Harry. "I wonder what's in the wind," said the latter. "Johnson has gone, and now Lot wants to go. It will break us all up. Are they afraid to stay here, I wonder?"

That evening Harry Esmond went to the Blue Boar.

"What is all this, 'Jone,' about the disappearance of Holmes?"

Blue looked at him curiously. "You ought to know if any one does."

"But I don't," says Harry, "or I wouldn't have asked you."

Blue: "You know it was all settled that he had to be put out of the way. There was no other way to make ourselves safe."

"Yes, I know that; but none of our fellows know who did it. That's the queer thing about it. Our intention was good enough, but who has carried it out?"

"Don't Lot or Lynn know about it?" queried Jonas.

"They say not," replied Harry. "But Lynn has gone away and now Lot talks about wanting to move up on Bingamon. I don't understand it all."

"Would you think it possible," continued Esmond, after a little consideration, as if he did not quite like to make the suggestion, "that these two could have come across George somewhere by accident and dispatched him and concluded to keep it a secret from the rest?"

"If they thought he had a few dollars in his pocket, they might. You know $10 would be a prize to either of them."

"You know George came home just after New Year's," remarked Harry.

"Yes, and it wouldn't be strange if he started to go down to your house to see Loraine," remarked Blue.

"That would be very probable," said Harry. "When Johnson was going away," he resumed, "he said he thought this was a good place to be away from; and Lot said a change of pasture was good for sheep, when he told old Nickie about wanting to move away."

"It looks as if they were afraid of something," said Blue.

"It does, for a fact."

CHAPTER XXXIV.

GIVEN UP BY THE RIVER.

It is a wise father that knows his own child.
—Shakespeare.

One Sunday morning in March, a horseman came into the village from below by the Fairmont pike and turning up Ferry street rode up to the Holmes residence and dismounted. One of the daughters was on the porch and walked towards him with inquiring looks as he came forward. He asked if this was where Mr. Holmes lived and she answered, yes.

"I am afraid I have sad news for you," he said.

The girl divined on the instant that it was something about her missing brother, and her heart stood still.

"A body was found this morning in the river at Worthlesston," the man went on, "and knowing George is missing, people there think it may be his."

The mother, who had been standing just within the door, had heard the conversation and stepped out on the porch as these words were spoken. "O, my God!" she screamed and fell insensible. Mr. Holmes, hearing the commotion, came out and the stranger repeated his statement to him while the girl went to the assistance of her mother. "I am not surprised," he said, calmly. "It is no more than I expected. I will get my horse and go with you."

At Worthlesston, a lad named Price had after breakfast walked down to the river bluff, which along the village front lies rather low. The recent freshets had deposited a good deal of drift on top of the bluff, and he was picking his way over this and looking down in an idle way into drifts that had in some places accumulated along the river's edge. He came to a large tree which, undermined by the current, had toppled into the river and, being held by the roots, had been swept around near the shore. Among the branches of the tree his eyes caught something that looked like a cast-off garment just showing above the water. With idle curiosity he walked out on the body of the tree and climbing down one of the large limbs was able to reach the object that had caught his attention. He thought it looked like a man's coat, and taking hold of it to lift it out of the water, found it resisted the effort, but answering the pull, the body of a man came to the surface and turned over, showing him the face horribly swollen, distorted and mutilated. The lad, shocked and frightened, quickly got back to the shore and gave the alarm. A crowd soon gathered, a skiff was procured and the body towed to a landing place and drawn out on the shore. Boards were procured, a hasty stretcher improvised and the body carried to the platform in front of the Martin house, where it was laid to await official inquiry.

William Good, coroner, empaneled a jury, who now only awaited the return of the messenger with Mr. Holmes.

George Holmes had been well known in the village and all knew of his disappearance two months before. The condition and especially the mutilation of the face made recognition impossible, but the presumption was it was the body of Holmes. A suggestion was raised whether this might not be the stranger who was supposed to have been murdered the time the stray horse was found, but it was not seriously entertained.

When Jacob Holmes, with drawn features and red but tearless eyes, came forward to look at the body, the crowd drew back respectfully to make way. He paused before the unsightly spectacle, all that was left as he supposed of his own son; looked at the face—what was left of it—long and anxiously; at the hair; at the clothing. The hair was matted and filled with mud and something that appeared to be coal dust. The clothing was so filled and covered with the mud and slime of the river it was hard to discern the texture of the cloth, still less its color. The flesh was so swollen and decayed recognition unless by some special mark was impossible; and it looked as if the mutilation of the features had been intentional. The old man looked long and doubtfully and seemed for a time to lose himself in revery. At length he said: "This looks like a coat that George wore about a year ago; the buttons and the binding are the same; but it was not the coat he had on when he went away. I hardly know what to think. It must be George, but no one can tell. That is about all I can say."

The jury found that the deceased, who was to them unknown, had come to his death from causes undiscovered. Mr. Holmes believing, and the coroner concurring, that it was the body of his son, was allowed to take the remains for burial. They were taken to Riverside, directly to the grave, and buried in the old graveyard on the hill overlooking the river, over against the great hill on the other side then known as the Lot Dyson hill, where Mr. Holmes believed his son had met his death.

There was a good deal of excitement in Riverside over the finding of the body, but it resulted in nothing. Very few, if any, doubted that it was Holmes. It was open to doubt in the minds of some whether he had been accidentally drowned or foully dealt with and thrown in the river. The appearance of coal grime in the hair gave color to the latter opinion.

There was one more who was deeply, painfully, interested in the finding of this body. When the word of George's disappearance was brought to the house by Ray Harris, it was the subject of mysterious, sometimes whispered, conversations about the house. The family all understood it was a blow to Loraine and avoided speech with her on the subject, and took care she should not hear what they said among themselves. Though startled by the report, she had felt no real alarm, relying on the words of his farewell letter which had prepared her for just such news. But when she got the word two months later of the finding of the body at Worthlesston, she was frightened. She did not hear it till after the burial. Then she went straight to George's family and had long and tearful interviews with the mother and sisters and with Mr. Holmes. He was the only one of the family that admitted any doubts.

He admitted it was impossible to identify the body as George's, and he was puzzled by the only other thing that could have furnished a clue, the clothing. His conviction arose more from corroborative circumstances than from evidence furnished by the corpse. Loraine knew, what she could not mention, that Hooker had disappeared in that vicinity a few days before George. Why might not this body be his? To try to comfort the Holmes family, she showed them the letter George had sent her the day before his disappearance. They hoped she might be right in her belief in his safety, but they were not convinced, for if this were not George's body whose was it? That was a question she dared not answer; and they settled down to an acceptance of George's death as the sorrowful truth.

CHAPTER XXXV.

PRINCE BOUNTIFUL.

A fellow feeling makes one wondrous kind.
—Garrick.

The time is a week after the last interview between Jonas Blue and Harry Esmond; the place the old Despard resort in Clarksburg; the personae, Lynn Johnson, Elias Tarbert and Abe Keifer. They are not playing but strolling around looking on at the game. They have just sat down in a corner, out of ear-shot, and putting their heads together begin a confidential talk.

"I didn't see Hooker," remarks Keifer, "as he came back, but I hear he went through by Esmonds'. A friend told me his job panned out well."

"He seemed in fine spirit at Esmonds," says Johnson. "He got there just in time for the Christmas dinner and left the next evening. He rode that last horse you sent down, Eli, and was to market him and send back the money."

"I hope he will hurry it along," said Tarbert, laughingly. "Times are pretty hard with me."

"I could lend you a little, if you really need it."

"I wish you would," returns Tarbert. "I expect to meet some friends here tomorrow and I would like to treat them white, and you know it takes money to do it."

"Would a fifty do you?" asks Johnson, with the air of a millionaire, thrusting finger and thumb into his vest pocket.

"You make my head swim," laughs Tarbert.

Johnson takes a roll from his vest pocket and drawing from it a $50 bill hands it to Tarbert, who looks at it incredulously, as if the transaction could not be real. "This is not 'queer', is it?" laughing again.

"When you are in luck and I am in need," pursues Johnson, loftily, "you can give it back to me."

Keifer looks on surprised. He had never seen Johnson with so much money. "You seem to be flush," he observes to Lynn in a jocular way.

"You know I have an income from my estates in Spain," says Johnson, gravely.

"In your mind," laughs Keifer.

"Now, boys," says Johnson, with a business air, "I have come into this country just to get you two together. Things are dull down our way. Harry is laying off and is not disposed to undertake anything fresh, and the rest of us have got to do something on our own account or starve."

"You won't starve," says Keifer, "as long as your pockets are lined with $50 bills like that one."

"How are you fixed, Abe?" asks Johnson, to whom it just occurs that Keifer does not seem quite happy. "Are you hard up, too?"

"Well, the fact is," replies Keifer, a trifle embarrassed, "I really am. I had thought of asking you to lend me a ten, but Eli got there first and I didn't like to ride a free horse too hard."

Johnson takes out the roll again and extracts from it another fifty and lays it in Keifer's palm. "This is the privilege of a friend," he says, grandly. "You may be flush sometime when I am broke; and, besides, it isn't fair to discriminate between friends."

"I hope to be able to return this before long," remarks Keifer, to pass the matter off a little more gracefully.

"Just what I want to plan for," says Johnson. "We three ought not to separate until we have found a place where we can collect some revenue. Now what do you say?"

With heads drawn closer together, and occasional furtive glances around to see if they were observed or could be overheard, the conference went on for a long time. At last they went out to the bar, took a drink all around at Johnson's expense and left the place.

CHAPTER XXXVI.

ENFRANCHISEMENT.

Who would be free themselves must strike the blow.
—Byron.

The struggle George Holmes went through that night at the ferry with the river before him and the skiff providentially at hand to carry him whither he would, was over the question whether he should cross the river for one more visit to Loraine, or at once, taking the boat as a means put in his way, go straight down the river to the promised land for which he was looking. His purpose had wavered wildly during the few minutes of his hesitation. The approach of the ferryman had precipitated a decision; for no sooner did he find himself in mid-stream, with a good boat beneath his feet, than his original purpose came back to him in all its strength. He remembered he had said to Loraine he would go the moment he found the means and would not see her again. Here was the means at his hand. If his resolution was ever to be good for anything he must keep it now. He had only to let the river carry him. Now if ever he must put aside everything but the one purpose to which he was pledged by all he held dear.

He trimmed the boat to the swift current, and dipping the oars with arms nerved with new hope and energy, sent it swiftly down the stream. The river had fallen considerably, as he could see on the shores, sometimes dimly visible in the starlight, but it was still high enough to carry him smoothly over all the dams. He was a good boatman, not afraid of the water; and he had his wages in his pocket.

And now there was nothing but a few hours between him and a new life, with security and the whole world before him from which to wrest fortune and reward. He was gliding swiftly towards that land of freedom, indexed by the North star, towards which many a fugitive with black skin had turned his longing eyes. To him it meant freedom, too, although his skin was white; for he was running away from the slavery of crime and degradation to a land where, God helping him, he meant to find the enfranchisement of a better life. Running away, too—he could not forget—from her who was more to him than all the rest of the world, than life itself; who embodied all that he loved, hoped for, was going to work for; from whom—strange paradox—he must run away as the only possible means of his ever being united to her!

A mile below, he passed the great elm and saw it towering giant-like between him and the sky. He could not see the old house beyond, but his thoughts went out to her under its roof who he felt must be at that moment thinking of him; whom it might be years before he could see—whom he might never see again; and he registered a fresh vow to rescue her from the accursed place at the earliest hour Heaven would let him.

CHAPTER XXXVII.

CLOSING ACCOUNTS.

Our acts our angels are, or good or ill,
Our fatal shadows that walk by us still.
—John Fletcher.

The storm has burst. The shot that was heard around the world has been fired at Sumter. Its reverberations have rolled from Charleston Harbor to the Golden Gate, and back to the piney woods of Maine. Abraham Lincoln has called for men to defend the integrity of the Federal Union, and nobly has the call been responded to.

May brought the first invasion of the "sacred soil" by the "Lincoln hirelings," who came to coerce the sovereign Old Dominion into obedience to the national authority. They crossed the Ohio at Parkersburg and advanced over the Baltimore & Ohio Railroad to Grafton, dropping a detachment at the old Harrison County town as a point of important strategic value. The secessionists of Clarksburg hastily retired before the advance of General Morris' troops and sought safety within Porterfield's lines at Phillippa. Away from the railroad numerous nests of other secessionists were organizing to join the Southern army. One of these was at Peter B. Righter's, some four miles east of Riverside, where men were nightly gathered and drilled by John Righter, who afterwards became the captain of a guerrilla band in the Rebel service. Union neighbors of the Righter farm became alarmed at these demonstrations and went to the commandant at Clarksburg with their complaint. A company of Ohio troops was sent down to the place. They burned the Righter homestead, broke up the rendezvous and struck a wholesome terror through all that region.

The Esmonds were as bitter secessionists as the Righters, and their place was rapidly becoming another rallying point for gathering recruits for the Confederate army. The example made of the Righter place put a summary stop to the work. It warned them what they might expect if complaint should be carried to Clarksburg, and they became alarmed. The Righters, father and son, had adroitly escaped arrest and made their way through the Confederate lines; but others might not be so successful; and the Esmonds knew they had other than political reasons for avoiding the possibility of arrest. In the event of military interference, there was no assurance St. George or Bernard might not appear on the ground and prosecute a search that they had not yet dared attempt.

Harry Esmond saw the time he had looked forward to had come. The neighborhood was too hot for him. So after one more visit to his friend of the Blue Boar, who was thoroughly frightened at the outlook, and quietly securing on his person a considerable sum of money he had been keeping in a safe place, he one night mounted his horse, bade the family adieu, and accompanied by Dyson, rode away—up the river, out of the neighborhood, and out of this history save what is related in another paragraph.

When Dyson bade good-bye to the elder Esmond he said:

"I told you, Uncle Nickie, sheep had to have a change of pasture sometimes."

"Well, Lot, keep a sharp lookout for sheep-killing dogs," was the old man's reply.

Some years after the war the writer of these pages learned, from a source entitled to be believed, that Harry Esmond, under another name, was living in the French Creek Valley, in Upshur County, West Virginia; that he had married there and was pursuing the life of a quiet, law-abiding citizen.

When the Third West Virginia Mounted Infantry was on service near Bulltown and Salt Lick Bridge, in October, 1863, where they had been fighting a force believed to be under the command of Jackson, horse-thieves made a raid on Capt. Roane's company and ran off a dozen of their best horses. Pursuit was made by Lieut.

Clarke, with a detachment of picked men, and with such success that the thieves, who were finding their market within the Confederate lines, were overtaken in Webster County, while eating breakfast around their camp fire. A volley from the pursuers brought down, killed or wounded, all the gang but one, who escaped; and among the killed, Clarke and several of his men, who were from Clarksburg, recognized our old friends Dyson and Johnson. True to their thievish instincts and habits they had been following their old trade along the border between the armies; but they had tempted fate once too often and had at last met the summary justice that had been looking for them many a year.

George Holmes, who had stopped for a time at Brownsville, was drawn by the growing excitement to Pittsburgh, with other young men who shared with him the universal indignation and patriotic ardor of that time. He joined them in enlistment in the Thirteenth Pennsylvania three-months men, Col. Rowley.

Holmes seemed transformed by the crisis and the occasion. There was an energy about him that could not but attract attention. Nothing was too much trouble for him; no work too hard. He had gone into the service with all his might, and in all he did was driven by a motive so imperious that it seemed to endow him with new faculties and an energy that knew no exhaustion. He set himself with diligence to learn the manual of arms, all the duties of camp and drill, the evolutions of the field—everything connected with his new functions as a soldier. He became so proficient that he was often set to drilling the company and was soon marked for promotion. But the three months expired before the regiment got into the active field. He went back to Pittsburgh and promptly reenlisted in a company organized by the Brownsville man who had befriended him when he landed there. This man had been a friend of his father in the old times, had received George into his home, and now in the organization of his company was abble to start him with the rank of first lieutenant.

The company was mustered into the Sixty-first Pennsylvania, Col. Rippey; a regiment that made a brilliant and memorable record, passing through the engagements of Opequon, Fisher's Hill, Cedar Creek, Antietam, Gettysburg, Fair Oaks, Malvern Hill, Cold Harbor, Spottsylvania, Wilderness, Petersburg. Holmes shared all the fortunes of this noble regiment, fighting with conspicuous bravery in the most hotly contested fields; yet except a slight wound at Fisher's Hill, which could not drive him from the field, he went through the war without a scratch. His captain and friend fell in the Wilderness and Holmes was made Captain.

The term of the regiment expired in September, 1864; but the "veterans," of whom Holmes was one, were retained till the close of the war, and not mustered out till June, 1865.

Ardent a soldier as Holmes had been, not one of all the million of men who laid down their arms was more eager than he to get away from Washington, where the regiment was disbanded.

Prior to this Jacob Holmes, broken by misfortune, had sold out and removed to the more thriving town of Massingham, on the Baltimore & Ohio railroad, which afterwards became an oil center and place of business importance. The family had been there but a short time when they received from Loraine a letter she had from George, telling her he had just closed his three years in the Union army and reenlisted for the war. He said the end of his term seemed to mark a period that entitled him to let her know where he was and what he was doing. He asked that she would communicate with his family and write him at once all that had occurred since he left. To the stricken family this was like a message from the dead; but they had long since learned to keep their own counsel and did not repeat the happy news outside their own relatives.

The information that George received in return showed him that the change in himself and in his fortunes was not the only change time had wrought. He could now go back to the old place and to Loraine without danger of assassination or other interference; and even had there been danger, it was nothing to him now, with his larger manhood and firmer purpose.

Years after the close of the civil war, the writer of these pages was carried by the currents of life and business to Pittsburgh, and was resident in the smoky metropolis for many subsequent years. While there he became well acquainted with the gentleman who figures in this history as Allan St. George.

St. George was caught up in the whirlwind of patriotic wrath that swept the northern states and cities after the firing on Sumter. He went into the army, with some of his office associates, to the neglect, it is to be regretted, of more than one duty like the search for McKinney, which had to give way before the grander duty that summoned men to the field of conflict. He came out of the war with the loss of a limb but with a star on his shoulder and an honored name.

In an exchange of reminiscences, he mentioned once his detective experiences in the upper Monongahela valley, and inquiry brought out the story detailed in these chapters, which fitted in wonderfully with the rest of the history known to the writer.

He was married, prosperous, happy, with a lovely wife and a luxurious home; and yet when he talked of Loraine Esmond it was plain to be seen that the finest and sweetest aspiration of his life had been lost with her, and that he treasured as his sacredest memory the picture of rare womanhood she had shown him.

It is a cruel fate that brings together and separates forever two souls so fitted for each other as these. In Loraine, St. George had awakened all that was sweetest and best in an exalted nature. She felt how gracious and stimulating life with such a man would be; yet she resolutely accepted the impossibility of it for her and respected the obligations she had assumed towards another, to whom her faith and duty had been pledged beyond recall. The more exhilarating life which the graces of St. George had given her a glimpse of was for others. It was only a "might have been" for her. She closed the door forever on everything but the memory of him; but she paid him, as we shall see, the highest tribute a woman can pay to the man who has touched her heart.

How few mortals, man or woman, marry their ideals! How many accept life, as Loraine did, on a level lower than their best, sighing vainly for the sweeter existence that, like the costliest wines, is reserved for the few who dwell on the heights and are favored of the gods!

Inexplicable are these bloodless tragedies of our lives. Why are the apparent purposes of the divinity within us thwarted? Is it because we need this chastening hand—because it is not best for us to be too happy? Is it because the "divine despair" that comes of this kind of disappointment chastens the bereaved souls with a culture more exquisite than could be wrought by the realization of the ideal and of perfect fruition? Who knows? There are mysteries of existence that lie deeper in the infinite purpose than the plummet of human wisdom has yet sounded.

CHAPTER XXXVIII.

LATER DISCOVERIES.

Stone walls do not a prison make,
Nor iron bars a cage.
—Lovelace.

Unknelled, uncoffined and unknown.
—Byron.

Years after Harry Esmond had disappeared from the homestead at the great elm, the place was sold, whether under financial pressure or for other reasons does not appear, and the family which yet remained together removed to a place some miles lower down the river. The new owner, a man of means and business thrift (announcement of whose death at an advanced age comes to hand in a local paper even as these pages are being written) proceeded to put the farm in good condition.

The place embraced what had been three farms all fronting along the river. The middle of one ran back and included a great hill with a ridge extending to the river, and along its abrupt and rugged face the river road had been cut and maintained with difficulty. Immediately above the road the cutting had exposed one of the deep coal measures that abound in this region; and here for several years coal was taken out for the dwellings of proprietor and tenants, until a room had been run nearly a hundred feet under the hill.

The new owner was struck by the accessibility of this old mine, the depth of the vein and the quality of the coal. With a couple of lanterns and a hired man he one day entered on an exploration. Save a little fall of earth and rock at the mouth the mine was clear back to the end of the cutting. When they came near enough to see the end wall, they were about to retrace the way when happening to walk a little farther they discovered that the cutting turned to the north. Following this up, they soon came in sight of the wall and were about to conclude again that this was the end of it, when turning to the right they found the wall on that side again disappeared. Turning again into this angle they proceeded twenty-five or thirty feet and this time found the termination of the cutting.

They found some other things that surprised them. They were in what appeared to be a deserted stable. There were evidences that horses had been quartered there. Posts were set against the end wall, wedged tightly between roof and floor, with hitching rings in them, to one of which still hung an old leathern halter, white with mildew and decay. There were rough mangers with the discolored remains of hay and weeds in them. A little distance back, against the side walls, were two rude benches which from their shape and width appeared to have been used for bunks. There were blocks that had probably served for seats, and there was the half-decayed seat and legs of a wooden chair. There was also on one side a rude structure of boards that had served the purposes of a table, and in an auger-hole in one corner of this was still a piece of tallow candle. Two posts set up with a cross-piece with nails had probably served as a hall-tree for coats and possibly for saddles and bridles.

The coal vein rose slightly as it receded from the river. A little groove in the floor along one wall had been cut to carry the seepage back to the turn, which being carried across to the outer room, kept the stable and the mine thoroughly drained.

The owner who made these discoveries was a discreet man. He knew the reputation of the farm before he bought it, and had got it cheap because of its ill repute. He understood the significance of this secret den, but saw nothing to be gained by making his discoveries public. He cautioned the man not to speak of what they had found and gave up the thought of reopening the mine. But the hired man felt the burden of the secret and found relief in dividing it with a friend, who in like manner passed it along till it ceased to be a secret.

The next season that part of the farm known as the "Dyson place" came in for a cleaning up The thicket referred to in these chapters was cut away and the ruins of the ancient house and the abandoned well were disclosed. It occurred to the owner that this well might be serviceable in dry seasons for watering stock, so one day the hired men were set to work to clean it out. Before the water had all been dipped out it became so offensive that an investigation was made to discover the reason. A grab hook was procured and soon brought up the remains of a human body, the bones and hair being still intact, the rotting clothing dropping to pieces as it came up. Horrified the men went for the proprietor; who, after satisfying himself as to the character of the discovery, directed them to return the remains to the well and to bring a team and fill it with earth. This was done and to-day the kindly turf hides from all recognition the spot where lie buried from all contemporary knowledge what are probably the remains of one who disappeared from earthly precincts more than one-third of a century ago. The men were cautioned not to mention the grewsome discovery and for a good while kept it to themselves. But such things cannot be buried by those who have no interest in their concealment, and in time the discovery became public property.

CHAPTER XXXIX.

REUNITED.

Across the hills and far away
  Beyond their utmost purple rim,
And deep into the dying day,
  The happy princess followed him.
—Day Dream.

Six years have rolled their circuits around the dial of time since the close of the war and the assassination of Lincoln. The great conflict seems already remote. The scars of battlefields that belong to history have been concealed by the gentle hand that hides us all in earth's oblivion at last. The men who put away the weapons of offense have taken up the occupations of peace and concord. The wounds of affection, the sorrows of desolated homes, under the soothing ministries of time, are healing into benign cicatrices. Eyes that were dim with bereavement are relighting with cheerfulness and hope.

We pick up the thread of our story on the west bank of the Neosho river, in the beautiful valley of that name, in sight of the thriving town of Neosho Falls, in Southeastern Kansas. In that mellow land, the season is well advanced. From the vast plain that stretches away to the west and southwest—to the foothills of the Rockies, to the margin of the Rio Grande, to the sands of the gulf—comes up the delicious breath of Spring, odorous with delights from

> "—that sweet South
> That breathes upon a bank of violets,"

Tree, grass, herbage and flower inhale the glad inspiration as they awaken from their winter torpor. The sweet-breathed kine, scattered over the swells and along the swales, crop the succulent grasses which nature's chemistry and the art of man convert into golden cream and butter for human delectation. The plowman is afield with sturdy team turning the sod that nature's alchemy will convert into gold for his coffers.

The sun sinks below the curve of the world and drops behind the western wilderness. The haze of the April evening broadens his benignant face and tempers his smile as, in a glow of crimson glory, he bids the earth good night. His last rays linger on a noble white elm that lifts its head beside the river where a well-kept farm, with a pretty cottage and neat farm buildings, bathes its feet in the glistening Neosho. The cottage stands facing the river, along whose margin a number of cottonwoods, great and small, seem to wait upon the greater elm, as faithful henchmen attend a chief.

In the rear door of this cottage stands a young, fresh, beautiful woman, with dark hair and lustrous brown eyes, whom we have seen before. The face is a little more rounded than of old; the eyes no brighter, no more alluring, but more contented and happy; the lips as sweet in their reserve, but not so sad in the droop of the cupid's bow, as in days gone by.

At her side is a lovely boy of some four summers whom we recognize as a duodecimo edition of the woman—the same brown eyes, the same dark locks, the same sweetness of mouth and strength of chin.

They are looking toward the plowed field whence the husband and father, his day's labor being ended, is driving his team to the barn. Now he is at the barn-yard gate, and the child shouts and dances with delight. In a few minutes more the farmer has ungeared and put away the horses, and comes toward the house with springy step, head erect and bright of eye. The little boy springs down the steps and runs along the path, is lifted and tossed in the air, and rides to the house on one shoulder, with arms clinging lovingly around his father's neck and calling to his mother to see his "horse." Loraine advances to meet them and to reward her husband's toil with the touch of her lips and the love in her eyes.

The farmer is a sturdy, almost stalwart, man whom we recognize despite the transformation wrought by time and ennobling purpose. He has grown and expanded in physical proportions as well as moral, and seems more stalwart than his inches would verify because of the manly, confident bearing that attends him. He is "Captain Holmes" to his Kansas neighbors and by them well respected.

After supper, they carry chairs and rugs out upon the front porch, for Loraine likes to look at the river and the elm. A few minutes later Uncle Andy Morrow, who owns the adjoining farm and who pioneered the way into this valley—and selected this quarter-section for George and Loraine because of the fine elm on the river bank—crosses the stile and comes on to the house, accompanied by a widowed daughter.

The little boy runs out to meet them and wins another ride to the porch. The old man sits down with the rest and the little fellow climbs on his knee and wants a story.

"What is your name, my little man?" asks Uncle Andy.

"O, you know."

"I used to know, but I forget. My memory is failing," says the old man, smiling tenderly at the child.

"George St. George Holmes," lisps the sweet, childish treble.

"Now what did you ask me for?" he demands.

"I like to hear you say it," replies Uncle Andy.

"Mamma likes to hear me say it, too," says the ingenuous child; "and when I say it for her she kisses me, and one time she cried."

The glowing sky fades in the darkening East, and silence, like a benediction, falls on the little group. They sit and look towards the river and the eyes of Loraine rest tenderly on the lofty elm; but beyond these their thoughts go out to the distant homes they left among the hills and valleys of Virginia—not all with regrets on the part of the young people, for to them it was a land of bondage and terror from which they have been delivered.

The little boy nestles his curls sleepily on Uncle Andy's breast, and Loraine draws her chair nearer to George's and lays her hand lovingly in his; and in the delicious stillness of the evening an unexpressed communion of thought, alternately sweet and painful, tempers their hearts to humility. With deep thankfulness, with love for one another and fondest affection for the young life entrusted to their keeping; with remembrance for all left behind, and pity for those who went astray and almost wrecked their lives; with mingled joy and sorrow; with hope and trust for the future—they sit long after the last twilight has withdrawn from the sky, until the kindly stars come out of its darkened depths and beam on them with a promise of happier days.

CPSIA information can be obtained
at www.ICGtesting.com
Printed in the USA
BVHW040427100921
616334BV00004B/232

9 781376 238563